OXFORD READINGS IN PHILOSOPHY

Series Editor G. J. Warnock

PHILOSOPHICAL LOGIC

PHILOSOPHICAL LOGIC

Edited by

P. F. STRAWSON

OXFORD UNIVERSITY PRESS

Oxford University Press, Ely House, London W. 1

GLASGOW NEW YORK TORONTO MELBOURNE WELLINGTON
CAPE TOWN IBADAN NAIROBI DAR ES SALAAM LUSAKA ADDIS ABABA
DELHI BOMBAY CALCUTTA MADRAS KARACHI LAHORE DACCA
KUALA LUMPUR SINGAPORE HONG KONG TOKYO

First published 1967
Reprinted 1968, 1973

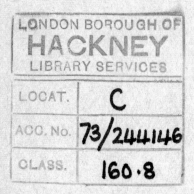
Filmset by St. Paul's Press, Malta
Printed in Great Britain
at the University Press, Oxford
by Vivian Ridler
Printer to the University

CONTENTS

INTRODUCTION

I

Formal and Philosophical Logic. We affirm or deny that p; wonder whether p; or think that if p, then q. It may be true that p; or it may not. From the supposition that p, there follows, or does not follow, the consequence that q.

If we use 'proposition' as a general name for what, when these forms are exemplified, we introduce or specify by such 'that'-, 'whether'- or 'if'-clauses, then logic is the general theory of the proposition. It has a formal part and a philosophical part. The aims and concerns of the formal science of logic are various, though interrelated; but one quite basic aim is the systematic presentation of certain relations of deducibility or implication which hold among propositions. The formal logician is not concerned with the entire field of deducibility relations. He is concerned only with such of them as hold among the members of groups of propositions when, and because, the members of such a group collectively exhibit certain structural or formal features. These features are represented in the logician's science by sets of schemata or logical skeletons of the kind with which every student of elementary logic is familiar. The schemata with which such a student is most familiar nowadays are, speaking roughly, made up of logical constants (or logical particles) on the one hand and sentence-letters, predicate-letters and variables on the other.

Wittgenstein, in the *Tractatus*, seems to suggest that the whole of formal logic—or at least the calculus of truth-functions and the predicate-calculus—is really implicit in the single idea of a proposition in general, that it could in principle be excogitated by pure reflection on this idea alone.[1] Wittgenstein's suggestion does not itself belong to formal logic. It belongs to philosophical logic. For it is, or may be, the beginning of an answer to some typical questions asked in philosophical logic: viz., What is really distinctive of the forms and constants of logic? or, What general elucidatory account can be given of the notion of a logical particle?

[1] See *Tractatus Logico-Philosophicus*, 5.47. (See Bibliography for all publications whose details are not given in the footnotes to this Introduction.)

Each of the notions so far introduced forms the topic of a similar question asked in philosophical logic. What, exactly, is a *proposition*? What is meant by saying that a proposition is *true*? What, in general, is the nature of that relation which holds between propositions when one *follows from*, or is *deducible from*, another? The attempt to find satisfying answers to these questions forces the philosopher to ask many others, about the nature and functioning of language and of linguistic expressions of many types. For propositions cannot be a subject of study unless they are expressed; and formal logic would have none but a purely mathematical interest unless it were related to actual discourse. So many questions concerning modes of actual discourse, the theory of meaning, the nature and conditions of linguistic communication, come within the scope of the philosophical logician's inquiries.

It seems characteristic of all these questions that they exhibit a high degree of interdependence: the adoption of an answer, or a method of approach, to one carries commitments to related answers, to similar methods of approach, to others. It is a tenable, though more debatable, thesis that the philosophical logician's questions are also inextricably intertwined with others, which are conventionally assigned to different branches of philosophy; that the theory of the proposition cannot really be separated from the theory of knowledge or the theory of being. It is certain, at least, that the initial approach to these questions can be made from very different directions. One philosophical logician will take the current system of formal logic itself as the firm base from which to direct all his ordering operations against the unruly tribes of language, all his explanatory manoeuvres among the diverse phenomena of speech. Another will start—as far away as possible from this base—by examining those phenomena themselves in all their particularity and detail.[1] Will the true order be achieved when the adherents of both approaches are folded in a single party, when we have a theory of meaning firm enough and rich enough to accommodate in a single, unified account both the simplicity of logical laws and the diversity of linguistic phenomena? Perhaps it will—if there is such a thing as the true order.

[1] Cf. J. L. Austin, *How To Do Things With Words*, Lecture XII, p. 147: "The total speech act in the total speech situation is the *only actual* phenomenon which, in the last resort, we are engaged in elucidating."

II

The general propositional form. At any rate, we can begin to order the questions. Let us take as our starting-point that dictum of Wittgenstein's which I have already alluded to: "One could say that the sole logical constant was what *all* propositions, by their very nature, had in common with one another. But that is the general propositional form."[1] Elsewhere he says that the general propositional form is: This is how things are.[2]

Clearly Wittgenstein does not mean that there is literally only one logical constant. He must be taken to mean, as I have already suggested, that the forms and constants of logic are somehow implicit in the bare notion of a proposition in general. If this is so, some steps are needed to show that it is so. Such steps can be taken, even if, in taking them, we do not tread exactly in Wittgenstein's own.

Propositions are of different kinds and figure in discourse in different ways. The propositions with which Wittgenstein in the *Tractatus*, in common with all men at most times, was fundamentally concerned were propositions about how things are in the world we live in; and one fundamental way in which such propositions figure in discourse is by being asserted. We *say* that this is how things are.

Among propositions of this fundamental kind we can in turn distinguish a fundamental subclass to which belong most of the propositions we are day by day concerned with. If we are to be able to say how things are in the world, we must have at our disposal the means of doing two complementary things, of performing two complementary functions: we must be able to specify *general types* of situation, thing, event etc. and we must be able to attach these general specifications to *particular cases*, to indicate their particular incidence in the world. Austin acknowledges this necessity in his own way when he says that two types of convention are necessary to the possibility of our saying things about the world: descriptive conventions correlating words with general types of situation etc. and demonstrative conventions correlating words (as uttered on particular occasions) with particular situations to be found in the world.[3] When Kant says that the possibility of our having empirical knowledge

---

[1] *Tractatus*, 5.47.

[2] *Tractatus*, 4.5.

[3] 'Truth', *Philosophical Papers*, pp. 89–90. But his way is open to objection. See P. F. Strawson, 'Truth: a Reconsideration of Austin's Views', *Philosophical Quarterly* (1965).

depends on our having both particular intuitions and general concepts, it is precisely the same necessary duality which he is acknowledging, only transposed, as it were, from the logical into the epistemological key.

A certain asymmetry is to be noticed between these dual and complementary functions. If I attach a general character to a particular chunk of the world, then there are certain other general characters which I thereby exclude from that chunk of the world; but there are not (in general) certain other chunks of the world which I thereby exclude from that general character. If I characterize a particular surface as red, I implicitly exclude, as unrealized, the possibility of that particular surface being blue; but I do not similarly exclude the possibility of any other particular surface being red. This asymmetry is of importance to understanding the logical character of reference and predication. But for the moment we are less concerned with the asymmetrical distribution of the excluding power in our fundamental kind of assertion than with the fact and necessity of the existence of that power. The excluding power which belongs to general predicates in assertions of this kind must belong, in some way or other, to *every* assertion about the world we live in. If such an assertion is to be potentially informative, it cannot be compatible with any and every conceivable state of affairs whatever. If it excluded nothing, it would say nothing.

To say that every assertion about the world must admit of the two mutually exclusive possibilities of being true or being false[1] is simply to express the same point in another way. Human assertions do not *make* the world, as divine ordinances are said to do, and would not be assertions if they did. To characterize a particular surface as being red is not to exclude its being blue or green in the way in which to paint it red is to exclude its being blue or green. It is to exclude these and other such possibilities in just the way which creates for the assertion itself the mutually exclusive possibilities of being a true or a false assertion.

In thus presenting some essential properties of a fundamental kind of assertion, one is at the same time presenting some essential properties of a fundamental kind of proposition. For whatever is asserted is a proposition and whatever is a proposition is assertible, though it can also figure in thought or discourse in other ways than the way of

---

[1] It should be noticed that this is not—or not obviously—to say that every such assertion must actually possess one or other of the two mutually exclusive truth-values. Thus a controversial issue is avoided, or at least postponed.

assertion, as, e.g., in some subordinate or co-ordinate clauses. The order of presentation may be seen simply as a matter of convenience; or it may be seen as something more. The point is arguable, but will not be argued now.

For now we have taken enough steps. We have at our disposal the notions of specifying the general type and attaching it to the particular case. We also have at our disposal the notion of every proposition's admitting of the two mutually exclusive possibilities of truth and falsity. And, at least as regards the current logic of truth-functions and quantification, we need nothing more. The idea of a plurality of propositions, each the possible possessor of one of the two mutually exclusive truth-values, truth and falsity, carries with it the idea of different possible combinations of these truth-values for pairs or sets of propositions. Nothing more is needed for the explanation of the force of those forms or schemata which represent different modes of truth-functional composition. Again, the idea of specifying a general type and attaching it to a particular case carries with it the idea of a range of propositions in which the same general concept is applied to a plurality of different particular cases. If we combine the notion of such a range with the thought of every proposition as the possible possessor of one of the two mutually exclusive truth-values, truth or falsity, we obtain once more the thought of different possible combinations of truth-values among the members of such a set of propositions. Many of such combinations, of course, will include *at least one case of truth*. The thought of a linguistic form or schema representing this last idea is, precisely, the thought of the existentially quantified form.

III

Reference and Predication. This rough gloss on Wittgenstein's dictum serves to connect together some of the notions the philosophical logician is concerned with; but it may be felt to leave them all rather in the air. One way of bringing them down to earth is to inquire how, in our ordinary linguistic practice, we set about attaching our specifications of general types to the particular case. There is in fact no single simple means by which we perform this operation. The duality of function—general specification, particular attachment—is not mirrored in some simple duality of linguistic conventions or expression-types. There are deep enough reasons why it should not be, deep enough reasons why the simplest of the typical commonplace sentences in which we make such assertions about how things are seem to offer themselves for division in a way which does not reflect precisely ·the duality I have spoken of, but another, though related, duality: that of reference and predication. We join together expressions which serve to identify particular items in the world with expressions which serve to classify them or characterize them in respect of some temporary or standing state or relation. But the referring part of our sentence in general contributes also to the specification of the general types of situation ostensibly reported—if it is an assertion we are making—and the predicative part may include also indications of where and when in the world the situation is to be found.

Expressions of different types, among which proper names have a peculiar and deserved prominence, are used to perform the function of identifying reference to particular items in the world. How exactly they do this; under what conditions; in what ways things can go wrong, and what the consequences are of their going radically wrong—these are matters of obscurity and discussion. They are also matters about which it is hard to become clear without importing considerations—regarding the context and purpose of discourse, the intentions and assumptions of speakers, the equipment and interest of audiences—which seem far removed from the serene abstractness of formal logic. Moreover, expressions of the types concerned appear in some contexts in which they cannot be cast at all for the simply identifying role, and in others in which they play the role with such a difference as, misunderstood, will generate paradox. Further careful attention to extra-formal considerations is needed here. But to some formally-minded logicians—above all, perhaps, to Quine—the difficulties surrounding reference have seemed, rather, to supply a motive for its elimination from an ideally intelligible language, theoretically adequate for all our purposes, in which existential quantification alone shall be available to declare the instantiation of general types, and universal quantification, with identity, to declare uniqueness, while all the rest of the burden normally carried by our referring expressions is transferred into predicate-position, where it can do (it is hoped) no harm. By the same stroke, the troubling concept of existence is to be exhibited in its true character.

In the notation of current logic the distinction between singular reference and predication is given a fundamental place, even though, if Quine's recommendations were followed, referring position would always be captured by the bound variables of quantification. This distinction was introduced above in terms of the distinction between the *identification* and the *characterization* of particular items in the world, of spatio-temporal individuals; and this mode of introduction provides a basis for analogical explanation of the fact that items other than spatio-temporal particulars may figure in our propositions as identified subjects of predication.

Such an account of reference and predication may be found objectionable, however, on the ground that it imports extra-logical impurities into a notion belonging essentially to logic. Perhaps some such thought underlies the suggestion that the distinction consists simply in this: that we can negate a singular proposition by negating its predicate but not by negating its subject.[1] Now some such asymmetry may hold indeed. But we should surely want to know *why* it holds. We can begin to see why, if we reflect once more on the distinction between the identification and the characterization of a particular individual. I have already remarked upon the asymmetry between these in respect of exclusion. In every case in which a general character is ascribed to a particular identified individual, there is a complementary general character or range of characters the possession of which, or of any one of which, by the identified individual would be incompatible with its possession of the ascribed character; but there is not (in general) any complementary particular individual or range of individuals the possession by which, or by any of which, of the ascribed character would be incompatible with the identified individual's possession of that character. Hence character-ascribing expressions have complementaries, and individual-identifying expressions do not. Hence we can produce a negation of a singular predication by negating the predicate (character-ascribing expression); but there is not, in general, any comparable operation we can perform upon the subject (individual-identifying expression).[2]

IV

Truth-functions and Conditionals. The forms and particles of current logic may be, as Wittgenstein suggested, excogitatable by pure reflection on the general nature of the proposition. This by itself gives no reason why every unitary particle belonging to the system should

[1] Cf. P. T. Geach, *Reference and Generality*, chapter 2; also 'Assertion', *Philosophical Review* (1965).

[2] The question is more complicated than is here suggested. These are only hints.

have a precise correlate in the resources of actual discourse. What we find *there* will turn on the general needs and purposes of speech. Now, in fact, within the system of logic itself, it is not found worthwhile to introduce a special symbol for, e.g., every possible mode of truth-functional composition of pairs of propositions. In fact, several symbols actually introduced into truth-functional logic display a more or less close correspondence to certain unitary expressions of common speech. And of course there is really nothing surprising about this. Though the current system might have sprung entire from archangelic meditation on the concept of a proposition, it came in fact, more laboriously, through refinement on natural language, through a progressively profounder insight into structures discernible within, or behind, it.

There is one important case in which the question of how close the correspondence is between a truth-functional form and its natural analogue cannot be regarded as settled. The 'if . . . then . . .' form of ordinary speech and writing obviously plays a role of major importance in reasoning and argument. Is its meaning preserved in the material conditional ('. . . ⊃ . . .') of logic?

Some might dispute the importance of the question on the ground that there is no series of formal deductive steps we could ever consistently and usefully take in which 'if . . . then . . . ' and ' . . . ⊃ . . . ' could not be safely interchanged. But the philosopher of logic will be too acutely aware of the ramifications of the question to dismiss it on this ground.

Those who argue that the full meaning of 'if' is not preserved by the truth-functional connective may point to what seems to them an analogous difference between the meaning of 'so' (or 'hence' or 'consequently') and the meaning of 'and'. One who asserts something of the form '*p*, so *q*' does more than assert the truth of the conjoined propositions. He is committed, by the very meaning of the linking conjunction, to implying the existence of some relation of a ground-consequent kind between the matters asserted in the two conjoined clauses. Could there not be a conjunction conventionally carrying a similar implication regarding the propositions it links, but differing from 'so' in that it is conventionally restricted to conjoining propositions which remain unasserted in any use made of the sentence containing the conjunction? If there were such a conjunction, we should have plenty of occasion for using it. Is there any reason for denying that 'if . . . then . . . ' is just such a conjunction?

Some logicians would say that there was reason for denying this;

or, at least, would deny that there was adequate reason for
affirming it. Thus Quine: "Such connection between antecedent
and consequent underlies the useful application of the conditional
without needing to participate in its meaning. Such connection underlies the useful application of the conditional even though the
meaning of the conditional be understood precisely as '-(p.-q)'.[1] Some
of those who show themselves thus disposed to take a truth-function-
alist view of the meaning of 'if . . . then . . . ' in the case of conditional
assertions made in contexts in which the truth-value of antecedent
and consequent is regarded as an open question (open conditionals)
seem to waver in the face of conditional assertions of another class,
where the *falsity* of the antecedent is taken for granted (counterfactual conditionals). But if the case is to be made at all, it must be
made boldly. The least attractive of all possible views is that 'if . . .
then . . . ' has one meaning in the context of an open conditional and
another and different meaning in the case of the corresponding
counterfactual conditional.

The debate over the meaning of 'if . . . then . . . ' is not an isolated
struggle; nor is the field even of that struggle restricted to the 'truth-
functionalist' and 'consequentialist' contenders. On the one hand,
Quine's (perhaps fairly casually made) distinction between the 'useful
application' and the 'meaning' of the conditional form seems to
invite a more general consideration of the relations between meaning
and use. On the other, the very notion of trying to settle *the* meaning
of the form may invite scepticism.

V

Meaning and Use. To know the meaning (or meanings) of a sentence of a
language is to be at least partially equipped to understand how any
serious utterance of it by a particular speaker in a particular context
is to be taken. But evidently to grasp the whole of what should be
taken to be intended to be understood by such an utterance is
generally something more than merely to know the meaning of the
words uttered. Somewhere in between grasping the former and
knowing the latter comes the ability to identify any *propositions* actually
expressed in the making of the utterance. It comes in between the
two, on the one hand, because sentence-meaning alone, without help
from the context of utterance, will rarely reveal just at what points

[1] *Methods of Logic*, p. 16. The case has been most powerfully argued by Grice in
a paper unfortunately unpublished.

the general concepts which figure in a proposition are there conceived as attaching to the world; and, on the other, because knowledge merely of what proposition is expressed does not include knowledge of how its expression is to be taken, or of all it is to be taken to imply. If, then, we speak of the whole of what may properly be taken to be intended to be understood by the making of a particular utterance as the *force* of that utterance, we have the trio: force, proposition(s) expressed (if any), sentence-meaning. And we have the problem of determining the precise relations between them.

Austin attacked one part of this problem, distinguishing certain general *types* of force which utterances may have, and calling attention, in the theory of the explicit performative, to kinds of sentence-structure which allow general types of force to be made explicit through sentence-meaning. Implicit in the distinctions he drew was the hint, more relevant to our immediate concerns, that in our zealous philosophical pursuit of the uses to which words may be put, the forces with which they may be employed, we may be tempted into a mistaken identification of the meanings of certain words with elements in the force of certain types of utterance in which those words are commonly used.

Here a great field of controversy lies open. It may be argued, on the one hand, that the philosophical aim is essentially that of *systematic* comprehension, and that this purpose is best served by a principled austerity in the distinction of meanings and types of meaning, supplemented by a sustained effort to explain the varieties of use as the result of an interplay between austerely conceived meanings on the one hand and the general or particular purposes of discourse on the other. Into the execution of such a programme there may well enter an element of legislation, both as regards 'meaning' and as regards other words. (Quine's attempt to enlist 'if . . . then . . . ' in the regiment of truth-functional connectives is at least in the spirit of such a programme.) At the opposite extreme there stands a scepticism, perhaps characteristic of the later Wittgenstein, which questions the very notion of definite, nuclear meanings and offers instead the picture of more or less loosely connected members of a family of uses. Between the extremes there is room for moderate men to steer a course inclining now in this direction, now in that.

VI

Meaning and Necessity. Between sentence-meaning and utterance-force there comes, sometimes, the proposition. The notion of propositional identity, which includes at least the notions of identity of reference and identity of sense, seems at first sight to be one which a formal logician must take for granted in all his reasonings. Recurrences of sentence-letters, predicate-letters and name-variables are no less essential than the symbols for logical constants if sets of schemata are to exhibit those structural features on which formal deducibility relations depend. Pre-occupied with the elaboration of a formal system, a logician need not inquire too closely what these recurrences actually represent. Concerned with its application, he must. It does not seem enough to say that such recurrences represent repetitions of sentences, predicate-expressions and names. For such repetitions do not guarantee identities of reference, sense and proposition.[1]

I have already remarked how some logicians, faced with the complexities of identifying reference, would eliminate the function altogether from the ideally intelligible language. It is perhaps more surprising that the notion of sense and, with it, the notion of a proposition itself, should inspire a similar revulsion. But these notions are bound up with others, prominent among them those of *necessary* truth and *necessary* consequence, of logical or conceptual *possibility* and *impossibility*, which to some formally-minded logicians (Quine, Goodman) seem opaque, even though others, no less formally-minded (Carnap, Church), find them perfectly acceptable. In glossing Wittgenstein's dictum about logical constants, I drew heavily upon ideas of this class; and perhaps it is because no general characterization is available which altogether eschews them that Quine, in explaining the notion of logical truth, offers a definition which rests, in the end, on a mere listing of logical particles.[2]

Ultimately, readiness to accept these ideas turns on readiness to accept, as genuine and irreducible, a distinction between questions of meaning and questions of fact. At an earlier phase in the discussion of necessary truth, a different issue seemed to divide opinion: was the fact that a sentence expressed a necessary truth, or that a proposition expressed by one sentence followed necessarily from the proposition expressed by another, something which was ensured merely by the meanings of the sentences concerned or did it reflect some further kind of super-fact differing from an ordinary fact in its unalterable necessity? This phase of debate is ended. Super-facts

---

[1] See P. F. Strawson, 'Propositions, Concepts and Logical Truth', *Philosophical Quarterly* (1957).

[2] 'Two Dogmas of Empiricism', *From a Logical Point of View*, p. 22–23.

are seen to be superfluous; and the meanings of sentences expressing necessary propositions are acknowledged, by those who believe there are such propositions, to be enough to guarantee their necessity.

What of the non-believers? For the distinction between questions of meaning and questions of fact is substituted an undifferentiated notion of truth, roughly to be understood in terms of the acceptability, in the face of experience, of sentences in context. Though some sentences, and some classes of sentences, are more securely rooted than others, none in principle enjoys the kind of special status assigned by believers to the imaginary class of necessary truths. Any sentence can be abandoned, any can be preserved—so long as we are prepared to make such adjustments elsewhere as are required to secure consistency in the system of accepted sentences.

This last proviso, however, induces doubts about the consistency of the non-believers' own doctrine. Why should the admission of one sentence require the rejection of another? Does not this mean that at least some sentences (e.g. some conditional sentences) at least some-times express propositions having the status of necessary truths? The non-believer may explain that no such compulsions are absolute, that it is simply that some sentences, e.g. truths of current logic, are much more deeply rooted in our acceptance-system than others. But this reply does not begin to touch the objection. The question is why there should be any limitations *at all* on admissible combinations of beliefs or (should the word 'beliefs' be found objectionable) on admissible combinations of accepted sentences.

The non-believer has a further reply, though it may be one that he is reluctant to give. He may say that such limitations and compulsions exist indeed, though not as matters of meaning and necessity (as understood by his opponents). They exist as matters of psychological or sociological fact. It is simply a matter of natural fact that we feel unable to accept certain combinations of sentences and that we should be at a loss and not know how to act unless we experienced some such inhibitions and compulsions. Or—to distance ourselves still further from the phenomena—there exist observable patterns of rejection- and acceptance-behaviour in relation to combinations of sentences, and the utility of language to its users seems to depend upon the existence of such patterns of behaviour.

These remarks, at their own level, may be true enough. They represent a point of view which we can perhaps adopt for part of the time; but not one which we can occupy for all, or much, of the time. For we are language-users before we are, or can be, (comprehending) observers of language-use; and as language-users we do not merely experience compulsions, but know what we mean by what we say, well enough at least to recognize (some) inconsistencies and consequences attributable solely to the sense of what is said. Certain concessions can, indeed, freely be made to the non-believers. We can admit that the meanings of many important expressions are relatively indeterminate, so that at a given moment there may be no answer to the question whether a given sentence containing such an expression expresses a necessary truth or not. We can admit that any expression may suffer a *change* of meaning, and some sentence containing it a consequent change of status. We can admit intelligible oddities of usage, prompted perhaps by oddities of circumstance, such that what seems prima facie a contradiction is no such thing, or that a consequence which would normally seem to follow from something does not follow at all. We can admit, in general, an intimate interplay between concept, fact and language. And perhaps these concessions are enough to pacify the non-believer. If so, we must point out to him that they turn on the admission of distinctions which he officially rejects.

VII

Truth. Frege said that the word 'true' indicates the object of logic as 'beautiful' does that of aesthetics and 'good' that of ethics.[1] Certainly the concept seems to be inseparably connected with every topic which has so far been mentioned. Yet, if Ramsey is right, there is very little to be said about the meaning of the word 'true'. Ramsey's very little is roughly this: that every proposition in which 'true' is predicated is equivalent to the proposition it is predicated of.[2] This has seemed too little. Why predicate 'true' at all if this is the whole truth? And what of the cases in which 'true' is predicated of propositions which the speaker cannot specify?

Truth is predicated *of* propositions, and a proposition is something which is, or might be, propounded, either in the way of assertion or in some other way, and is, or might be, thought or supposed, whether propounded or not. The difference between saying, e.g., 'If p, then . . .' and saying 'If it is true that p, then . . .' is that in the latter case we show

---

[1] See 'The Thought: A Logical Inquiry', included in this volume.

[2] The relevant passage, from 'Facts and Propositions', *Proceedings of the Aristotelian Society*, Supp. Vol. (1927), is reprinted in '*Truth*', ed. Pitcher (Prentice-Hall, 1964), pp. 16–17.

ourselves thinking of the proposition that *p* as something that may be (or has been) propounded or thought independently of our current expression of it, and hence as a possible *subject* of predication. We could approximate our sense, depending on the case, by something like 'If, as has been (may be) thought (said), *p*, then . . .'. In general, then, when 'true' is predicated, there is an allusion to an actual or possible propounding or thinking of some proposition. The small modification of Ramsey's doctrine, which this calls for shows clearly enough how to approximate the sense of predications of 'true' both of propositions which the speaker does not specify in the predication and of propositions which he cannot. The general propositional form is: This is how things are. Hence, for 'If what he says is true, then . . .' we have 'If things are as he says they are, then . . .'. Not knowing what the prophetess will predict, we may say: 'Whatever she may predict, if her prediction turns out true, then I will sacrifice to the god'; and for this we have: 'Whatever her prediction may be, if things turn out as she predicts, then I will sacrifice to the god.'

To this account of 'true' we may add, if we choose, observations regarding its utility in common discourse, its availability, for example, as a convenient abbreviatory device, for acts of confirming, conceding, admitting etc.—even though we thereby risk prompting a somewhat gratuitous urging of the *nouvelle vague* injunction, 'Don't look for the use, look for the meaning'.

If this still seems too little for a Theory of Truth, the title may properly be allowed to stand, where it has often stood, at the head of other, related investigations: into the kinds of conventional relations which hold between words and world when true propositions are expressed; into the nature of belief, or judgement, that some proposition is true; or into the kinds of condition which justify holding such beliefs.[1]

VIII

Categories. We commonly think of the range of exclusion of a given predicate, and hence of the coverage of the negation of that predicate, as restricted in certain ways. We think of 'not green' as in logical competition with 'green' in much the same way as we think of 'blue' as in logical competition with 'green', of 'not more than thirty years old' as disputing for place with 'more than thirty years old'

---

[1] See P. F. Strawson, 'A Problem about Truth—a Reply to Mr. Warnock', *Truth*, ed. Pitcher, p. 84.

much as 'less than thirty years old' does. The negative phrase seems to be merely the most tolerant, because the least specific, member of the class of colour-predicates which compete with 'green' or of age-predicates which compete with 'more than thirty years old'.

So we may freely think on almost all our occasions. But there are some occasions, both frivolous and serious, on which we are prepared to think of negative predication in a more extended style. In the game of guessing what someone is thinking of, he may reply to a question: 'No, it is not green (not more than thirty years old)', when what he is thinking of is not a visual object or has no age at all, e.g. when he is thinking of a number. Or, in philosophy, striving to correct what seems to us some radical misconception or to emphasize some radical difference, we may try to make our point more vivid by attaching the negation of some relatively specific predicate to the designation of something which, it seems, in its very nature, cannot possess any of the predicates which we normally think of as belonging to the exclusion-range of the predicate we choose. His heart is beneath his ribs, but his soul is not beneath his ribs. He tore up the report; but he did not tear up the facts.

Thus we may try to convey a sense of conceptual disparateness by exploiting a sense of absurdity. It is not, it seems, *merely* false that he tore up the facts. It is absurd to suppose that, in a literal sense, he might have. Facts are not the sort of thing that can be, literally, torn up.

Is it possible to present a clear and general distinction between predications which are false in *this* way of absurdity and predications which are false because of the possession by their subjects of characteristics belonging to the normal exclusion range of the predicate, when the predicate is taken in a certain sense and taken literally in that sense? To ask this is as much as to ask whether we can give a clear and general account of the notion of the normal exclusion range of a predicate, taken in a certain sense and taken literally in that sense. The fact that we can give some examples of predicates for which it is easy to specify such a range does not, of course, mean that the general notion is, or can be made, clear.

Some philosophers have taken it for granted that the distinctions in question are clear, or are capable of being made so.[1] Others have shown scepticism about this assumption or have argued against it.

---

[1] At least one has been willing, on the basis of such an assumption, to sketch the outline of a general logical doctrine of categories or types. See F. Sommers, 'Types and Ontology', included in this volume.

Those who find the notion of meaning in general opaque can scarcely be expected to find the notion of category-absurdity clear; but scepticism on this point is by no means confined to them. The issue—like some others more dogmatically handled in this brief sketch—may be regarded as open.

I

THE THOUGHT : A LOGICAL INQUIRY

Gottlob Frege

(translated by A. M. and Marcelle Quinton)

THE word 'true' indicates the aim of logic as does 'beautiful' that of aesthetics or 'good' that of ethics. All sciences have truth as their goal; but logic is also concerned with it in a quite different way from this. It has much the same relation to truth as physics has to weight or heat. To discover truths is the task of all sciences; it falls to logic to discern the laws of truth. The word 'law' is used in two senses. When we speak of laws of morals or the state we mean regulations which ought to be obeyed but with which actual happenings are not always in conformity. Laws of nature are the generalization of natural occurrences with which the occurrences are always in accordance. It is rather in this sense that I speak of laws of truth. This is, to be sure, not a matter of what happens so much as of what is. Rules for asserting, thinking, judging, inferring, follow from the laws of truth. And thus one can very well speak of laws of thought too. But there is an imminent danger here of mixing different things up. Perhaps the expression 'law of thought' is interpreted by analogy with 'law of nature' and the generalization of thinking as a mental occurrence is meant by it. A law of thought in this sense would be a psychological law. And so one might come to believe that logic deals with the mental process of thinking and the psychological laws in accordance with which it takes place. This would be a misunderstanding of the task of logic, for truth has not been given the place which is its due here. Error and superstition have causes just as much as genuine knowledge. The assertion both of what is false and of what is true takes place in accordance with psychological laws. A derivation from these and an explanation of a mental process that terminates in an assertion can never take the place of a proof of what is asserted. Could not logical laws also have played a part in this mental process?

From *Mind*, Vol. 65 (1956), pp. 289–311. Reprinted by permission of the translators, A. M. and Marcelle Quinton, and the Editor of *Mind*.

I do not want to dispute this, but when it is a question of truth possibility is not enough. For it is also possible that something not logical played a part in the process and deflected it from the truth. We can only decide this after we have discerned the laws of truth; but then we will probably be able to do without the derivation and explanation of the mental process if it is important to us to decide whether the assertion in which the process terminates is justified. In order to avoid this misunderstanding and to prevent the blurring of the boundary between psychology and logic, I assign to logic the task of discovering the laws of truth, not of assertion or thought. The meaning of the word 'true' is explained by the laws of truth.

But first I shall attempt to outline roughly what I want to call true in this connexion. In this way other uses of our word may be excluded. It is not to be used here in the sense of 'genuine' or 'veracious', nor, as it sometimes occurs in the treatment of questions of art, when, for example, truth in art is discussed, when truth is set up as the goal of art, when the truth of a work of art or true feeling is spoken of. The word 'true' is put in front of another word in order to show that this word is to be understood in its proper, unadulterated sense. This use too lies off the path followed here; that kind of truth is meant whose recognition is the goal of science.

Grammatically the word 'true' appears as an adjective. Hence the desire arises to delimit more closely the sphere in which truth can be affirmed, in which truth comes into the question at all. One finds truth affirmed of pictures, ideas, statements, and thoughts. It is striking that visible and audible things occur here alongside things which cannot be perceived with the senses. This hints that shifts of meaning have taken place. Indeed! Is a picture, then, as a mere visible and tangible thing, really true, and a stone, a leaf, not true? Obviously one would not call a picture true unless there were an intention behind it. A picture must represent something. Furthermore, an idea is not called true in itself but only with respect to an intention that it should correspond to something. It might be supposed from this that truth consists in the correspondence of a picture with what it depicts. Correspondence is a relation. This is contradicted, however, by the use of the word 'true', which is not a relation-word and contains no reference to anything else to which something must correspond. If I do not know that a picture is meant to represent Cologne Cathedral then I do not know with what to compare the picture to decide on its truth. A correspondence, moreover, can only be perfect if the corresponding things coincide and are, therefore, not distinct things at all. It is said to be possible to establish the authenticity of a bank-note by comparing it stereoscopically with an authentic one. But it would be ridiculous to try to compare a gold piece with a twenty-mark note stereoscopically. It would only be possible to compare an idea with a thing if the thing were an idea too. And then, if the first did correspond perfectly with the second, they would coincide. But this is not at all what is wanted when truth is defined as the correspondence of an idea with something real. For it is absolutely essential that the reality be distinct from the idea. But then there can be no complete correspondence, no complete truth. So nothing at all would be true; for what is only half true is untrue. Truth cannot tolerate a more or less. But yet? Can it not be laid down that truth exists when there is correspondence in a certain respect? But in which? For what would we then have to do to decide whether something were true? We should have to inquire whether it were true that an idea and a reality, perhaps, corresponded in the laid-down respect. And then we should be confronted by a question of the same kind and the game could begin again. So the attempt to explain truth as correspondence collapses. And every other attempt to define truth collapses too. For in a definition certain characteristics would have to be stated. And in application to any particular case the question would always arise whether it were true that the characteristics were present. So one goes round in a circle. Consequently, it is probable that the content of the word 'true' is unique and indefinable.

When one ascribes truth to a picture one does not really want to ascribe a property which belongs to this picture altogether inde-pendently of other things, but one always has something quite different in mind and one wants to say that that picture corresponds in some way to this thing. 'My idea corresponds to Cologne Cathedral' is a sentence and the question now arises of the truth of this sentence. So what is improperly called the truth of pictures and ideas is reduced to the truth of sentences. What does one call a sentence? A series of sounds; but only when it has a sense, by which is not meant that every series of sounds that has sense is a sentence. And when we call a sentence true we really mean its sense is. From which it follows that it is for the sense of a sentence that the question of truth arises in general. Now is the sense of a sentence an idea? In any case being true does not consist in the correspondence of this sense with something else, for otherwise the question of truth would reiterate itself to infinity.

Without wishing to give a definition, I call a thought something for which the question of truth arises. So I ascribe what is false to a thought just as much as what is true.[1] So I can say: the thought is the sense of the sentence without wishing to say as well that the sense of every sentence is a thought. The thought, in itself immaterial, clothes itself in the material garment of a sentence and thereby becomes comprehensible to us. We say a sentence expresses a thought.

A thought is something immaterial and everything material and perceptible is excluded from this sphere of that for which the question of truth arises. Truth is not a quality that corresponds with a particular kind of sense-impression. So it is sharply distinguished from the qualities which we denote by the words 'red', 'bitter', 'lilac-smelling'. But do we not see that the sun has risen and do we not then also see that this is true? That the sun has risen is not an object which emits rays that reach my eyes, it is not a visible thing like the sun itself. That the sun has risen is seen to be true on the basis of sense-impressions. But being true is not a material, perceptible property. For being magnetic is also recognized on the basis of sense-impressions of something, though this property corresponds as little as truth with a particular kind of sense-impressions. So far these properties agree. However, we need sense-impressions in order to recognize a body as magnetic. On the other hand, when I find that it is true that I do not smell anything at this moment, I do not do so on the basis of sense-impressions.

It may nevertheless be thought that we cannot recognize a property of a thing without at the same time realizing the thought that this thing has this property to be true. So with every property of a thing is joined a property of a thought, namely, that of truth. It is also worthy of notice that the sentence 'I smell the scent of violets' has just the same content as the sentence 'it is true that I smell the scent of violets'. So it seems, then, that nothing is added to the thought by my ascribing to it the property of truth. And yet is it not a great result when the scientist after much hesitation and careful inquiry, can

[1] In a similar way it has perhaps been said 'a judgement is something which is either true or false'. In fact I use the word 'thought' in approximately the sense which 'judgement' has in the writings of logicians. I hope it will become clear in what follows why I choose 'thought'. Such an explanation has been objected to on the ground that in it a distinction is drawn between true and false judgements which of all possible distinctions among judgements has perhaps the least significance. I cannot see that it is a logical deficiency that a distinction is given with the explanation. As far as significance is concerned, it should not by any means be judged as trifling if, as I have said, the word 'true' indicates the aim of logic.

finally say 'what I supposed is true'? The meaning of the word 'true' seems to be altogether unique. May we not be dealing here with something which cannot, in the ordinary sense, be called a quality at all? In spite of this doubt I want first to express myself in accordance with ordinary usage, as if truth were a quality, until something more to the point is found.

In order to work out more precisely what I want to call thought, I shall distinguish various kinds of sentences.[1] One does not want to deny sense to an imperative sentence, but this sense is not such that the question of truth could arise for it. Therefore I shall not call the sense of an imperative sentence a thought. Sentences expressing desires or requests are ruled out in the same way. Only those sentences in which we communicate or state something come into the question. But I do not count among these exclamations in which one vents one's feelings, groaning, sighing, laughing, unless it has been decided by some agreement that they are to communicate something. But how about interrogative sentences? In a word-question we utter an incomplete sentence which only obtains a true sense through the completion for which we ask. Word-questions are accordingly left out of consideration here. Sentence-questions are a different matter. We expect to hear 'yes' or 'no'. The answer 'yes' means the same as an indicative sentence, for in it the thought that was already completely contained in the interrogative sentence is laid down as true. So a sentence-question can be formed from every indicative sentence. An exclamation cannot be regarded as a communication on this account, since no corresponding sentence-question can be formed. An interrogative sentence and an indicative one contain the same thought; but the indicative contains something else as well, namely, the assertion. The interrogative sentence contains something more too, namely a request. Therefore two things must be distinguished in an indicative sentence: the content, which it has in common with the corresponding sentence-question, and the assertion. The former is the thought, or at least contains the thought. So it is possible to express the thought without laying it down as true. Both are so closely joined in an indicative sentence that it is easy to overlook their separability. Consequently we may distinguish:

---

[1] I am not using the word 'sentence' here in a purely grammatical sense where it also includes subordinate clauses. An isolated subordinate clause does not always have a sense about which the question of truth can arise, whereas the complex sentence to which it belongs has such a sense.

(1) the apprehension of a thought—thinking,
(2) the recognition of the truth of a thought—judgement,[1]
(3) the manifestation of this judgement—assertion.

We perform the first act when we form a sentence-question. An advance in science usually takes place in this way, first a thought is apprehended, such as can perhaps be expressed in a sentence-question, and, after appropriate investigations, this thought is finally recognized to be true. We declare the recognition of truth in the form of an indicative sentence. We do not have to use the word 'true' for this. And even when we do use it the real assertive force lies, not in it, but in the form of the indicative sentence and where this loses its assertive force the word 'true' cannot put it back again. This happens when we do not speak seriously. As stage thunder is only apparent thunder and a stage fight only an apparent fight, so stage assertion is only apparent assertion. It is only acting, only fancy. In his part the actor asserts nothing, nor does he lie, even if he says something of whose falsehood he is convinced. In poetry we have the case of thoughts being expressed without being actually put forward as true in spite of the form of the indicative sentence, although it may be suggested to the hearer to make an assenting judgement himself. Therefore it must still always be asked, about what is presented in the form of an indicative sentence, whether it really contains an assertion. And this question must be answered in the negative if the requisite seriousness is lacking. It is irrelevant whether the word 'true' is used here. This explains why it is that nothing seems to be added to a thought by attributing to it the property of truth.

An indicative sentence often contains, as well as a thought and the assertion, a third component over which the assertion does not extend. This is often said to act on the feelings, the mood of the hearer or to arouse his imagination. Words like 'alas' and 'thank God' belong here. Such constituents of sentences are more noticeably prominent in poetry, but are seldom wholly absent from prose. They occur more rarely in mathematical, physical, or chemical than in

---

[1] It seems to me that thought and judgement have not hitherto been adequately distinguished. Perhaps language is misleading. For we have no particular clause in the indicative sentence which corresponds to the assertion, that something is being asserted lies rather in the form of the indicative. We have the advantage in German that main and subordinate clauses are distinguished by the word-order. In this connexion it is noticeable that a subordinate clause can also contain an assertion and that often neither main nor subordinate clause express a complete thought by themselves but only the complex sentence does.

historical expositions. What are called the humanities are more closely connected with poetry and are therefore less scientific than the exact sciences which are drier the more exact they are, for exact science is directed toward truth and only the truth. Therefore all constituents of sentences to which the assertive force does not reach do not belong to scientific exposition but they are sometimes hard to avoid, even for one who sees the danger connected with them. Where the main thing is to approach what cannot be grasped in thought by means of guesswork these components have their justification. The more exactly scientific an exposition is the less will the nationality of its author be discernible and the easier will it be to translate. On the other hand, the constituents of language, to which I want to call attention here, make the translation of poetry very difficult, even make a complete translation almost always impossible, for it is in precisely that in which poetic value largely consists that languages differ most.

It makes no difference to the thought whether I use the word 'horse' or 'steed' or 'cart-horse' or 'mare'. The assertive force does not extend over that in which these words differ. What is called mood, fragrance, illumination in a poem, what is portrayed by cadence and rhythm, does not belong to the thought.

Much of language serves the purpose of aiding the hearer's understanding, for instance the stressing of part of a sentence by accentuation or word-order. One should remember words like 'still' and 'already' too. With the sentence 'Alfred has still not come' one really says 'Alfred has not come' and, at the same time, hints that his arrival is expected, but it is only hinted. It cannot be said that, since Alfred's arrival is not expected, the sense of the sentence is therefore false. The word 'but' differs from 'and' in that with it one intimates that what follows is in contrast with what would be expected from what preceded it. Such suggestions in speech make no difference to the thought. A sentence can be transformed by changing the verb from active to passive and making the object the subject at the same time. In the same way the dative may be changed into the nominative while 'give' is replaced by 'receive'. Naturally such transformations are not indifferent in every respect; but they do not touch the thought, they do not touch what is true or false. If the inadmissibility of such transformations were generally admitted then all deeper logical investigation would be hindered. It is just as important to neglect distinctions that do not touch the heart of the matter as to make distinctions which concern what is essential. But what is essential depends on one's purpose. To a mind concerned with what is beautiful in language what is indifferent to the logician can appear as just what is important.

Thus the contents of a sentence often go beyond the thoughts expressed by it. But the opposite often happens too, that the mere wording, which can be grasped by writing or the gramophone does not suffice for the expression of the thought. The present tense is used in two ways: first, in order to give a date, second, in order to eliminate any temporal restriction where timelessness or eternity is part of the thought. Think, for instance, of the laws of mathematics. Which of the two cases occurs is not expressed but must be guessed. If a time indication is needed by the present tense one must know when the sentence was uttered to apprehend the thought correctly. Therefore the time of utterance is part of the expression of the thought. If someone wants to say the same today as he expressed yesterday using the word 'today', he must replace this word with 'yesterday'. Although the thought is the same its verbal expression must be different so that the sense, which would otherwise be affected by the differing times of utterance, is readjusted. The case is the same with words like 'here' and 'there'. In all such cases the mere wording, as it is given in writing, is not the complete expression of the thought, but the knowledge of certain accompanying conditions of utterance, which are used as means of expressing the thought, are needed for its correct apprehension. The pointing of fingers, hand movements, glances may belong here too. The same utterance containing the word 'I' will express different thoughts in the mouths of different men, of which some may be true, others false.

The occurrence of the word 'I' in a sentence gives rise to some questions.

Consider the following case. Dr. Gustav Lauben says, 'I have been wounded'. Leo Peter hears this and remarks some days later, 'Dr. Gustav Lauben has been wounded'. Does this sentence express the same thought as the one Dr. Lauben uttered himself? Suppose that Rudolph Lingens were present when Dr. Lauben spoke and now hears what is related by Leo Peter. If the same thought is uttered by Dr. Lauben and Leo Peter then Rudolph Lingens, who is fully master of the language and remembers what Dr. Lauben has said in his presence, must now know at once from Leo Peter's report that the same thing is under discussion. But knowledge of the language is a separate thing when it is a matter of proper names. It may well be the case that only a few people associate a particular thought with the sentence 'Dr. Lauben has been wounded'. In this case one needs for complete understanding a knowledge of the expression 'Dr. Lauben'. Now if both Leo Peter and Rudolph Lingens understand by 'Dr. Lauben' the doctor who lives as the only doctor in a house known to both of them, then they both understand the sentence 'Dr. Gustav Lauben has been wounded' in the same way, they associate the same thought with it. But it is also possible that Rudolph Lingens does not know Dr. Lauben personally and does not know that he is the very Dr. Lauben who recently said 'I have been wounded.' In this case Rudolph Lingens cannot know that the same thing is in question. I say, therefore, in this case: the thought which Leo Peter expresses is not the same as that which Dr. Lauben uttered.

Suppose further that Herbert Garner knows that Dr. Gustav Lauben was born on 13th September, 1875 in N.N. and this is not true of anyone else; against this, suppose that he does not know where Dr. Lauben now lives nor indeed anything about him. On the other hand, suppose Leo Peter does not know that Dr. Lauben was born on 13th September 1875, in N.N. Then as far as the proper name 'Dr. Gustav Lauben' is concerned, Herbert Garner and Leo Peter do not speak the same language, since, although they do in fact refer to the same man with this name, they do not know that they do so. Therefore Herbert Garner does not associate the same thought with the sentence 'Dr. Gustav Lauben has been wounded' as Leo Peter wants to express with it. To avoid the drawback of Herbert Garner's and Leo Peter's not speaking the same language, I am assuming that Leo Peter uses the proper name 'Dr. Lauben' and Herbert Garner, on the other hand, uses the proper name 'Gustav Lauben'. Now it is possible that Herbert Garner takes the sense of the sentence 'Dr. Lauben has been wounded' to be true while, misled by false information, taking the sense of the sentence 'Gustav Lauben has been wounded' to be false. Under the assumptions given these thoughts are therefore different.

Accordingly, with a proper name, it depends on how whatever it refers to is presented. This can happen in different ways and every such way corresponds with a particular sense of a sentence containing a proper name. The different thoughts which thus result from the same sentence correspond in their truth-value, of course; that is to say, if one is true then all are true, and if one is false then all are false. Nevertheless their distinctness must be recognized. So it must really be demanded that a single way in which whatever is referred to is presented be associated with every proper name. It is often unimportant that this demand should be fulfilled but not always.

Now everyone is presented to himself in a particular and primitive way, in which he is presented to no-one else. So, when Dr. Lauben thinks that he has been wounded, he will probably take as a basis this primitive way in which he is presented to himself. And only Dr. Lauben himself can grasp thoughts determined in this way. But now he may want to communicate with others. He cannot communicate a thought which he alone can grasp. Therefore, if he now says 'I have been wounded', he must use the 'I' in a sense which can be grasped by others, perhaps in the sense of 'he who is speaking to you at this moment', by doing which he makes the associated conditions of his utterance serve for the expression of his thought.[1]

Yet there is a doubt. Is it at all the same thought which first that man expresses and now this one?

A person who is still untouched by philosophy knows first of all things which he can see and touch, in short, perceive with the senses, such as trees, stones and houses, and he is convinced that another person equally can see and touch the same tree and the same stone which he himself sees and touches. Obviously no thought belongs to these things. Now can he, nevertheless, stand in the same relation to a person as a tree?

Even an unphilosophical person soon finds it necessary to recognize an inner world distinct from the outer world, a world of sense-impressions, of creations of his imagination, of sensations, of feelings and moods, a world of inclinations, wishes and decisions. For brevity I want to collect all these, with the exception of decisions, under the word 'idea'.

Now do thoughts belong to this inner world? Are they ideas? They are obviously not decisions. How are ideas distinct from the things of the outer world? First:

Ideas cannot be seen or touched, cannot be smelled, nor tasted, nor heard.

I go for a walk with a companion. I see a green field, I have a visual impression of the green as well. I have it but I do not see it.

Secondly: ideas are had. One has sensations, feelings, moods,

---

[1] I am not in the happy position here of a mineralogist who shows his hearers a mountain crystal. I cannot put a thought in the hands of my readers with the request that they should minutely examine it from all sides. I have to content myself with presenting the reader with a thought, in itself immaterial, dressed in sensible linguistic form. The metaphorical aspect of language presents difficulties. The sensible always breaks in and makes expression metaphorical and so improper. So a battle with language takes place and I am compelled to occupy myself with language although it is not my proper concern here. I hope I have succeeded in making clear to my readers what I want to call a thought.

inclinations, wishes. An idea which someone has belongs to the content of his consciousness.

The field and the frogs in it, the sun which shines on them are there no matter whether I look at them or not, but the sense-impression I have of green exists only because of me, I am its bearer. It seems absurd to us that a pain, a mood, a wish should rove about the world without a bearer, independently. An experience is impossible without an experient. The inner world presupposes the person whose inner world it is.

Thirdly: ideas need a bearer. Things of the outer world are however independent.

My companion and I are convinced that we both see the same field; but each of us has a particular sense-impression of green. I notice a strawberry among the green strawberry leaves. My companion does not notice it, he is colour-blind. The colour-impression, which he receives from the strawberry, is not noticeably different from the one he receives from the leaf. Now does my companion see the green leaf as red, or does he see the red berry as green, or does he see both as of one colour with which I am not acquainted at all? These are unanswerable, indeed really nonsensical, questions. For when the word 'red' does not state a property of things but is supposed to characterize sense-impressions belonging to my consciousness, it is only applicable within the sphere of my consciousness. For it is impossible to compare my sense-impression with that of someone else. For that it would be necessary to bring together in one consciousness a sense-impression, belonging to one consciousness, with a sense-impression belonging to another consciousness. Now even if it were possible to make an idea disappear from one consciousness and, at the same time, to make an idea appear in another consciousness, the question whether it were the same idea in both would still remain unanswerable. It is so much of the essence of each of my ideas to be the content of my consciousness, that every idea of another person is, just as such, distinct from mine. But might it not be possible that my ideas, the entire content of my consciousness might be at the same time the content of a more embracing, perhaps divine, consciousness? Only if I were myself part of the divine consciousness. But then would they really be my ideas, would I be their bearer? This oversteps the limits of human understanding to such an extent that one must leave its possibility out of account. In any case it is impossible for us as men to compare another person's ideas with our own. I pick the strawberry, I hold it between my fingers. Now my companion sees it too, this very same strawberry; but each of us has his own idea. No other person has my idea but many people can see the same thing. No other person has my pain. Someone can have sympathy for me but still my pain always belongs to me and his sympathy to him. He does not have my pain and I do not have his sympathy.

Fourthly: every idea has only one bearer; no two men have the same idea.

For otherwise it would exist independently of this person and independently of that one. Is that lime-tree my idea? By using the expression 'that lime-tree' in this question I have really already anticipated the answer, for with this expression I want to refer to what I see and to what other people can also look at and touch. There are now two possibilities. If my intention is realized when I refer to something with the expression 'that lime-tree' then the thought expressed in the sentence 'that lime-tree is my idea' must obviously be negated. But if my intention is not realized, if I only think I see without really seeing, if on that account the designation 'that lime-tree' is empty, then I have gone astray into the sphere of fiction without knowing it or wanting to. In that case neither the content of the sentence 'that lime-tree is my idea' nor the content of the sentence 'that lime-tree is not my idea' is true, for in both cases I have a statement which lacks on object. So then one can only refuse to answer the question for the reason that the content of the sentence 'that lime-tree is my idea' is a piece of fiction. I have, naturally, got an idea then, but I am not referring to this with the words 'that lime-tree'. Now someone may really want to refer to one of his ideas with the words 'that lime-tree'. He would then be the bearer of that to which he wants to refer with those words, but then he would not see that lime-tree and no-one else would see it or be its bearer.

I now return to the question: is a thought an idea? If the thought I express in the Pythagorean theorem can be recognized by others just as much as by me then it does not belong to the content of my consciousness, I am not its bearer; yet I can, nevertheless, recognize it to be true. However, if it is not the same thought at all which is taken to be the content of the Pythagorean theorem by me and by another person, one should not really say 'the Pythagorean theorem' but 'my Pythagorean theorem', 'his Pythagorean theorem' and these would be different; for the sense belongs necessarily to the sentence. Then my thought can be the content of my consciousness and his thought the content of his. Could the sense of my Pythagorean theorem be true while that of his was false? I said that the word 'red' was applicable only in the sphere of my consciousness if it did not state a property of things but was supposed to characterize one of my sense-impressions. Therefore the words 'true' and 'false', as I understand them, could also be applicable only in the sphere of my consciousness, if they were not supposed to be concerned with something of which I was not the bearer, but were somehow appointed to characterize the content of my consciousness. Then truth would be restricted to the content of my consciousness and it would remain doubtful whether anything at all comparable occurred in the consciousness of others.

If every thought requires a bearer, to the contents of whose consciousness it belongs, then it would be a thought of this bearer only and there would be no science common to many, on which many could work. But I, perhaps, have my science, namely, a whole of thought whose bearer I am and another person has his. Each of us occupies himself with the contents of his own consciousness. No contradiction between the two sciences would then be possible and it would really be idle to dispute about truth, as idle, indeed almost ludicrous, as it would be for two people to dispute whether a hundred-mark note were genuine, where each meant the one he himself had in his pocket and understood the word 'genuine' in his own particular sense. If someone takes thoughts to be ideas, what he then recognizes to be true is, on his own view, the content of his consciousness and does not properly concern other people at all. If he were to hear from me the opinion that a thought is not an idea he could not dispute it, for, indeed, it would not now concern him.

So the result seems to be: thoughts are neither things of the outer world nor ideas.

A third realm must be recognized. What belongs to this corresponds with ideas, in that it cannot be perceived by the senses, but with things, in that it needs no bearer to the contents of whose consciousness to belong. Thus the thought, for example, which we expressed in the Pythagorean theorem is timelessly true, true independently of whether anyone takes it to be true. It needs no bearer. It is not true for the first time when it is discovered, but is like a planet which, already before anyone has seen it, has been in interaction with other planets.[1]

---

[1] One sees a thing, one has an idea, one apprehends or thinks a thought. When one apprehends or thinks a thought one does not create it but only comes to stand

But I think I hear an unusual objection. I have assumed several times that the same thing that I see can also be observed by other people. But how could this be the case, if everything were only a dream? If I only dreamed I was walking in the company of another person, if I only dreamed that my companion saw the green field as I did, if it were all only a play performed on the stage of my consciousness, it would be doubtful whether there were things of the outer world at all. Perhaps the realm of things is empty and I see no things and no men, but have only ideas of which I myself am the bearer. An idea, being something which can as little exist independently of me as my feeling of fatigue, cannot be a man, cannot look at the same field together with me, cannot see the strawberry I am holding. It is quite incredible that I should really have only my inner world instead of the whole environment, in which I am supposed to move and to act. And yet it is an inevitable consequence of the thesis that only what is my idea can be the object of my awareness. What would follow from this thesis if it were true? Would there then be other men? It would certainly be possible but I should know nothing of it. For a man cannot be my idea, consequently, if our thesis were true, he also cannot be an object of my awareness. And so the ground would be removed from under any process of thought in which I might assume that something was an object for another person as for myself, for even if this were to happen I should know nothing of it. It would be impossible for me to distinguish that of which I was the bearer from that of which I was not. In judging something not to be my idea I would make it the object of my thinking and, therefore, my idea. On this view, is there a green field? Perhaps, but it would not be visible to me. For if a field is not my idea, it cannot, according to our thesis, be an object of my awareness. But if it is my idea it is invisible, for ideas are not visible. I can indeed have the idea of a green field, but this is not green for there are no green ideas. Does a shell weighing a hundred kilogrammes exist, according to this view? Perhaps, but I could know nothing of it. If a shell is not my idea then, according to our thesis, it cannot be an object of my awareness, of my thinking. But if a shell were my idea, it would have no weight. I can have an idea of a heavy shell. This then contains the idea of weight as a part-idea. But this part-idea is not a property of the whole idea any more than Germany is a property of Europe. So it follows:

Either the thesis that only what is my idea can be the object of

in a certain relation, which is different from seeing a thing or having an idea, to what already existed beforehand.

my awareness is false, or all my knowledge and perception is limited to the range of my ideas, to the stage of my consciousness. In this case I should have only an inner world and I should know nothing of other people.

It is strange how, upon such reflections, the opposites collapse into each other. There is, let us suppose, a physiologist of the senses. As is proper for a scholarly scientist, he is, first of all, far from supposing the things he is convinced he sees and touches to be his ideas. On the contrary, he believes that in sense-impressions he has the surest proof of things which are wholly independent of his feeling, imagining, thinking, which have no need of his consciousness. So little does he consider nerve-fibres and ganglion-cells to be the content of his consciousness that he is, on the contrary, rather inclined to regard his consciousness as dependent on nerve-fibres and ganglion-cells. He establishes that light-rays, refracted in the eye, strike the visual nerve-endings and bring about a change, a stimulus, there. Some of it is transmitted through nerve-fibres and ganglion-cells. Further processes in the nervous system are perhaps involved, colour-impressions arise and these perhaps join themselves to what we call the idea of a tree. Physical, chemical and physiological occurrences insert themselves between the tree and my idea. These are immediately connected with my consciousness but, so it seems, are only occurrences in my nervous system and every spectator of the tree has his particular occurrences in his particular nervous system. Now the light-rays, before they enter my eye, may be reflected by a mirror and be spread further as if they came from a place behind the mirror. The effects on the visual nerves and all that follows will now take place just as they would if the light-rays had come from a tree behind the mirror and had been transmitted undisturbed to the eye. So an idea of a tree will finally occur even though such a tree does not exist at all. An idea, to which nothing at all corresponds, can also arise through the bending of light, with the mediation of the eye and the nervous system. But the stimulation of the visual nerves need not even happen through light. If lightning strikes near us we believe we see flames, even though we cannot see the lightning itself. In this case the visual nerve is perhaps stimulated by electric currents which originate in our body in consequence of the flash of lightning. If the visual nerve is stimulated by this means, just as it would be stimulated by light-rays coming from flames, then we believe we see flames. It just depends on the stimulation of the visual nerve, it is indifferent how that itself comes about.

One can go a step further still. This stimulation of the visual nerve is not actually immediately given, but is only a hypothesis. We believe that a thing, independent of us, stimulates a nerve and by this means produces a sense-impression, but, strictly speaking, we experience only the end of this process which projects into our consciousness. Could not this sense-impression, this sensation, which we attribute to a nerve-stimulation, have other causes also, as the same nerve-stimulation can arise in different ways? If we call what happens in our consciousness idea, then we really experience only ideas but not their causes. And if the scientist wants to avoid all mere hypothesis, then only ideas are left for him, everything resolves into ideas, the light-rays, nerve-fibres and ganglion-cells from which he started. So he finally undermines the foundations of his own construction. Is everything an idea? Does everything need a bearer, without which it could have no stability? I have considered myself as the bearer of my ideas, but am I not an idea myself? It seems to me as if I were lying in a deck-chair, as if I could see the toes of a pair of waxed boots, the front part of a pair of trousers, a waist-coat, buttons, part of a jacket, in particular sleeves, two hands, the hair of a beard, the blurred outline of a nose. Am I myself this entire association of visual impressions, this total idea? It also seems to me as if I see a chair over there. It is an idea. I am not actually much different from this myself, for am I not myself just an association of sense-impressions, an idea? But where then is the bearer of these ideas? How do I come to single out one of these ideas and set it up as the bearer of the rest? Why must it be the idea which I choose to call 'I'? Could I not just as well choose the one that I am tempted to call a chair? Why, after all, have a bearer for ideas at all? But this would always be something essentially different from merely borne ideas, something independent, needing no extraneous bearer. If everything is idea, then there is no bearer of ideas. And so now, once again, I experience a change into the opposite. If there is no bearer of ideas then there are also no ideas, for ideas need a bearer without which they cannot exist. If there is no ruler, there are also no subjects. The dependence, which I found myself induced to confer on the experience as opposed to the experient, is abolished if there is no more bearer. What I called ideas are then independent objects. Every reason is wanting for granting an exceptional position to that object which I call 'I'.

But is that possible? Can there be an experience without someone to experience it? What would this whole play be without an onlooker?

Can there be a pain without someone who has it? Being experienced is necessarily connected with pain, and someone experiencing is necessarily connected with being experienced. But there is something which is not my idea and yet which can be the object of my awareness, of my thinking, I am myself of this nature. Or can I be part of the content of my consciousness while another part is, perhaps, an idea of the moon? Does this perhaps take place when I judge that I am looking at the moon? Then this first part would have a consciousness and part of the content of this consciousness would be I myself once more. And so on. Yet it is surely inconceivable that I should be boxed into myself in this way to infinity, for then there would not be only one I but infinitely many. I am not my own idea and if I assert something about myself, e.g. that I do not feel any pain at this moment, then my judgement concerns something which is not a content of my consciousness, is not my idea, that is me myself. Therefore that about which I state something is not necessarily my idea. But, someone perhaps objects, if I think I have no pain at the moment, does not the word 'I' nevertheless correspond with something in the content of my consciousness and is that not an idea? That may be. A certain idea in my consciousness may be associated with the idea of the word 'I'. But then it is an idea among other ideas and I am its bearer as I am the bearer of the other ideas. I have an idea of myself but I am not identical with this idea. What is a content of my consciousness, my idea, should be sharply distinguished from what is an object of my thought. Therefore the thesis that only what belongs to the content of my consciousness can be the object of my awareness, of my thought, is false.

Now the way is clear for me to recognize another person as well as to be an independent bearer of ideas. I have an idea of him but I do not confuse it with him himself. And if I state something about my brother I do not state it about the idea that I have of my brother.

The invalid who has a pain is the bearer of this pain, but the doctor in attendance who reflects on the cause of this pain is not the bearer of the pain. He does not imagine he can relieve the pain by anaesthetizing himself. An idea in the doctor's mind may very well correspond to the pain of the invalid but that is not the pain and not what the doctor is trying to remove. The doctor might consult another doctor. Then one must distinguish: first, the pain whose bearer is the invalid, second, the first doctor's idea of this pain, third, the second doctor's idea of this pain. This idea does indeed belong to the content of the second doctor's consciousness, but it is not the object of his reflection, it is rather an aid to reflection, as a drawing can be such an aid perhaps.

Both doctors have the invalid's pain, which they do not bear, as their common object of thought. It can be seen from this that not only a thing but also an idea can be the common object of thought of people who do not have the idea.

So, it seems to me, the matter becomes intelligible. If man could not think and could not take something of which he was not the bearer as the object of his thought he would have an inner world but no outer world. But may this not be based on a mistake? I am convinced that the idea I associate with the words 'my brother' corresponds to something that is not my idea and about which I can say something. But may I not be making a mistake about this? Such mistakes do happen. We then, against our will, lapse into fiction. Indeed! By the step with which I secure an environment for myself I expose myself to the risk of error. And here I come up against a further distinction between my inner and outer worlds. I cannot doubt that I have a visual impression of green but it is not so certain that I see a lime-leaf. So, contrary to widespread views, we find certainty in the inner world while doubt never altogether leaves us in our excursions into the outer world. It is difficult in many cases, nevertheless, to distinguish probability from certainty here, so we can presume to judge about things in the outer world. And we must presume this even at the risk of error if we do not want to succumb to far greater dangers.

In consequence of these last considerations I lay down the following: not everything that can be the object of my understanding is an idea. I, as a bearer of ideas, am not myself an idea. Nothing now stands in the way of recognizing other people to be bearers of ideas as I am myself. And, once given the possibility, the probability is very great, so great that it is in my opinion no longer distinguishable from certainty. Would there be a science of history otherwise? Would not every precept of duty, every law otherwise come to nothing? What would be left of religion? The natural sciences too could only be assessed as fables like astrology and alchemy. Thus the reflections I have carried on, assuming that there are other people besides myself who can take the same thing as the object of their consideration, of their thinking, remain essentially unimpaired in force.

Not everything is an idea. Thus I can also recognize the thought, which other people can grasp just as much as I, as being independent of me. I can recognize a science in which many people can be engaged in research. We are not bearers of thoughts as we are bearers of our ideas. We do not have a thought as we have, say, a sense-impression, but we also do not see a thought as we see, say, a star. So it is advisable to choose a special expression and the word 'apprehend' offers itself for the purpose. A particular mental capacity, the power of thought, must correspond to the apprehension[1] of thought. In thinking we do not produce thoughts but we apprehend them. For what I have called thought stands in the closest relation to truth. What I recognize as true I judge to be true quite independently of my recognition of its truth and of my thinking about it. That someone thinks it has nothing to do with the truth of a thought. 'Facts, facts, facts' cries the scientist if he wants to emphasize the necessity of a firm foundation for science. What is a fact? A fact is a thought that is true. But the scientist will surely not recognize something which depends on men's varying states of mind to be the firm foundation of science. The work of science does not consist of creation but of the discovery of true thoughts. The astronomer can apply a mathematical truth in the investigation of long past events which took place when on earth at least no one had yet recognized that truth. He can do this because the truth of a thought is timeless. Therefore that truth cannot have come into existence with its discovery.

Not everything is an idea. Otherwise psychology would contain all the sciences within it or at least it would be the highest judge over all the sciences. Otherwise psychology would rule over logic and mathematics. But nothing would be a greater misunderstanding of mathematics than its subordination to psychology. Neither logic nor mathematics has the task of investigating minds and the contents of consciousness whose bearer is a single person. Perhaps their task could be represented rather as the investigation of the mind, of the mind not of minds.

The apprehension of a thought presupposes someone who apprehends it, who thinks. He is the bearer of the thinking but not of the thought. Although the thought does not belong to the contents of the thinker's consciousness yet something in his consciousness must be aimed at the thought. But this should not be confused with the thought itself. Similarly Algol itself is different from the idea someone has of Algol.

The thought belongs neither to my inner world as an idea nor yet to the outer world of material, perceptible things.

---

[1]The expression 'apprehend' is as metaphorical as 'content of consciousness'. The nature of language does not permit anything else. What I hold in my hand can certainly be regarded as the content of my hand but is all the same the content of my hand in quite a different way from the bones and muscles of which it is made and their tensions, and is much more extraneous to it than they are.

This consequence, however cogently it may follow from the exposition, will nevertheless not perhaps be accepted without opposition. It will, I think, seem impossible to some people to obtain information about something not belonging to the inner world except by sense-perception. Sense-perception indeed is often thought to be the most certain, even to be the sole, source of knowledge about everything that does not belong to the inner world. But with what right? For sense-impressions are necessary constituents of sense-perceptions and are a part of the inner world. In any case two men do not have the same, though they may have similar, sense-impressions. These alone do not disclose the outer world to us. Perhaps there is a being that has only sense-impressions without seeing or touching things. To have visual impressions is not to see things. How does it happen that I see the tree just there where I do see it? Obviously it depends on the visual impressions I have and on the particular type which occur because I see with two eyes. A particular image arises, physically speaking, on each of the two retinas. Another person sees the tree in the same place. He also has two retinal images but they differ from mine. We must assume that these retinal images correspond to our impressions. Consequently we have visual impressions, not only not the same, but markedly different from each other. And yet we move about in the same outer world. Having visual impressions is certainly necessary for seeing things but not sufficient. What must still be added is non-sensible. And yet this is just what opens up the outer world for us; for without this non-sensible something everyone would remain shut up in his inner world. So since the answer lies in the non-sensible, perhaps something non-sensible could also lead us out of the inner world and enable us to grasp thoughts where no sense-impressions were involved. Outside one's inner world one would have to distinguish the proper outer world of sensible, perceptible things from the realm of the non-sensibly perceptible. We should need something non-sensible for the recognition of both realms but for the sensible perception of things we should need sense-impressions as well and these belong entirely to the inner world. So that in which the distinction between the way in which a thing and a thought is given mainly consists is something which is attributable, not to both realms, but to the inner world. Thus I cannot find this distinction to be so great that on its account it would be impossible for a thought to be given that did not belong to the inner world.

The thought, admittedly, is not something which it is usual to call real. The world of the real is a world in which this acts on that, changes it and again experiences reactions itself and is changed by them. All this is a process in time. We will hardly recognize what is timeless and unchangeable as real. Now is the thought changeable or is it timeless? The thought we express by the Pythagorean theorem is surely timeless, eternal, unchangeable. But are there not thoughts which are true today but false in six months time? The thought, for example, that the tree there is covered with green leaves, will surely be false in six months time. No, for it is not the same thought at all. The words 'this tree is covered with green leaves' are not sufficient by themselves for the utterance, the time of utterance is involved as well. Without the time-indication this gives we have no complete thought, i.e. no thought at all. Only a sentence supplemented by a time-indication and complete in every respect expresses a thought. But this, if it is true, is true not only today or tomorrow but timelessly. Thus the present tense in 'is true' does not refer to the speaker's present but is, if the expression be permitted, a tense of timelessness. If we use the mere form of the indicative sentence, avoiding the word 'true', two things must be distinguished, the expression of the thought and the assertion. The time-indication that may be contained in the sentence belongs only to the expression of the thought, while the truth, whose recognition lies in the form of the indicative sentence, is timeless. Yet the same words, on account of the variability of language with time, take on another sense, express another thought; this change, however, concerns only the linguistic aspect of the matter.

And yet! What value could there be for us in the eternally unchangeable which could neither undergo effects nor have effect on us? Something entirely and in every respect inactive would be unreal and non-existent for us. Even the timeless, if it is to be anything for us, must somehow be implicated with the temporal. What would a thought be for me that was never apprehended by me? But by apprehending a thought I come into a relation to it and it to me. It is possible that the same thought that is thought by me today was not thought by me yesterday. In this way the strict timelessness is of course annulled. But one is inclined to distinguish between essential and inessential properties and to regard something as timeless if the changes it undergoes involve only its inessential properties. A property of a thought will be called inessential which consists in, or follows from the fact that, it is apprehended by a thinker.

How does a thought act? By being apprehended and taken to be true. This is a process in the inner world of a thinker which can have further consequences in this inner world and which, encroaching on the sphere of the will, can also make itself noticeable in the outer world. If, for example, I grasp the thought which we express by the theorem of Pythagoras, the consequence may be that I recognize it to be true and, further, that I apply it, making a decision which brings about the acceleration of masses. Thus our actions are usually prepared by thinking and judgement. And so thought can have an indirect influence on the motion of masses. The influence of one person on another is brought about for the most part by thoughts. One communicates a thought. How does this happen? One brings about changes in the common outside world which, perceived by another person, are supposed to induce him to apprehend a thought and take it to be true. Could the great events of world history have come about without the communication of thoughts? And yet we are inclined to regard thoughts as unreal because they appear to be without influence on events, while thinking, judging, stating, understanding and the like are facts of human life. How much more real a hammer appears compared with a thought. How different the process of handing over a hammer is from the communication of a thought. The hammer passes from one control to another, it is gripped, it undergoes pressure and on account of this its density, the disposition of its parts, is changed in places. There is nothing of all this with a thought. It does not leave the control of the communicator by being communicated, for after all a person has no control over it. When a thought is apprehended, it at first only brings about changes in the inner world of the apprehender, yet it remains untouched in its true essence, since the changes it undergoes involve only inessential properties. There is lacking here something we observe throughout the order of nature: reciprocal action. Thoughts are by no means unreal but their reality is of quite a different kind from that of things. And their effect is brought about by an act of the thinker without which they would be ineffective, at least as far as we can see. And yet the thinker does not create them but must take them as they are. They can be true without being apprehended by a thinker and are not wholly unreal even then, at least if they could be apprehended and by this means be brought into operation.

II

MEANING

H. P. GRICE

CONSIDER the following sentences:

'Those spots mean (meant) measles.'

'Those spots didn't mean anything to me, but to the doctor they meant measles.'

'The recent budget means that we shall have a hard year.'

(1) I cannot say, 'Those spots meant measles, but he hadn't got measles', and I cannot say, 'The recent budget means that we shall have a hard year, but we shan't have'. That is to say, in cases like the above, *x meant that p* and *x means that p* entail *p*.

(2) I cannot argue from 'Those spots mean (meant) measles' to any conclusion about 'what is (was) meant by those spots'; for example, I am not entitled to say, 'What was meant by those spots was that he had measles'. Equally I cannot draw from the statement about the recent budget the conclusion 'What is meant by the recent budget is that we shall have a hard year'.

(3) I cannot argue from 'Those spots meant measles' to any conclusion to the effect that somebody or other meant by those spots so-and-so. *Mutatis mutandis*, the same is true of the sentence about the recent budget.

(4) For none of the above examples can a restatement be found in which the verb 'mean' is followed by a sentence or phrase in inverted commas. Thus 'Those spots meant measles' cannot be reformulated as 'Those spots meant "measles"' or as 'Those spots meant "he has measles"'.

(5) On the other hand, for all these examples an approximate restatement can be found beginning with the phrase 'The fact that . . .'; for example, 'The fact that he had those spots meant that he had measles' and 'The fact that the recent budget was as it was means that we shall have a hard year'.

Now contrast the above sentences with the following:

From *Philosophical Review*, Vol. 66 (1957), pp. 377–88. Reprinted by permission of the author and the *Philosophical Review*.

'Those three rings on the bell (of the bus) mean that the bus is full.'

'That remark, "Smith couldn't get on without his trouble and strife", meant that Smith found his wife indispensable.'

(1) I can use the first of these and go on to say, 'But it isn't in fact full—the conductor has made a mistake'; and I can use the second and go on, 'But in fact Smith deserted her seven years ago'. That is to say, here *x means that p* and *x meant that p* do not entail *p*.

(2) I can argue from the first to some statement about 'what is (was) meant' by the rings on the bell and from the second to some statement about 'what is (was) meant' by the quoted remark.

(3) I can argue from the first sentence to the conclusion that somebody (viz., the conductor) meant, or at any rate should have meant, by the rings that the bus is full, and I can argue analogously for the second sentence.

(4) The first sentence can be restated in a form in which the verb 'mean' is followed by a phrase in inverted commas, that is, 'Those three rings on the bell mean "the bus is full"'. So also can the second sentence.

(5) Such a sentence as 'The fact that the bell has been rung three times means that the bus is full' is not a restatement of the meaning of the first sentence. Both may be true, but they do not have, even approximately, the same meaning.

When the expressions 'means', 'means something', 'means that' are used in the kind of way in which they are used in the first set of sentences, I shall speak of the sense, or senses, in which they are used, as the *natural* sense, or senses, of the expressions in question. When the expressions are used in the kind of way in which they are used, in the second set of sentences, I shall speak of the sense, or senses, in which they are used, as the *non-natural* sense, or senses, of the expressions in question. I shall use the abbreviation 'means$_{NN}$' to distinguish the non-natural sense or senses.

I propose, for convenience, also to include under the head of natural senses of 'mean' such senses of 'mean' as may be exemplified in sentences of the pattern '*A* means (meant) *to do* so-and-so (by *x*)', where *A* is a human agent. By contrast, as the previous examples show, I include under the head of non-natural senses of 'mean' any senses of 'mean' found in sentences of the patterns '*A* means (meant) something by *x*' or '*A* means (meant) by *x* that . . .' (This is over-rigid; but it will serve as an indication.)

I do not want to maintain that *all* our uses of 'mean' fall easily, obviously, and tidily into one of the two groups I have distinguished; but I think that in most cases we should be at least fairly strongly inclined to assimilate a use of 'mean' to one group rather than to the other. The question which now arises is this: 'What more can be said about the distinction between the cases where we should say that the word is applied in a natural sense and the cases where we should say that the word is applied in a non-natural sense?' Asking this question will not of course prohibit us from trying to give an explanation of 'meaning$_{NN}$' in terms of one or another natural sense of 'mean'.

This question about the distinction between natural and non-natural meaning is, I think, what people are getting at when they display an interest in a distinction between 'natural' and 'conventional' signs. But I think my formulation is better. For some things which can mean$_{NN}$ something are not signs (e.g., words are not), and some are not conventional in any ordinary sense (e.g., certain gestures); while some things which mean naturally are not signs of what they mean (cf. the recent budget example).

I want first to consider briefly, and reject, what I might term a causal type of answer to the question, 'What is meaning$_{NN}$?' We might try to say, for instance, more or less with C. L. Stevenson,[1] that for x to mean$_{NN}$ something, x must have (roughly) a tendency to produce in an audience some attitude (cognitive or otherwise) and a tendency, in the case of a speaker, to *be* produced *by* that attitude, these tendencies being dependent on 'an elaborate process of conditioning attending the use of the sign in communication'[2]. This clearly will not do.

(1) Let us consider a case where an utterance, if it qualifies at all as meaning$_{NN}$ something, will be of a descriptive or informative kind and the relevant attitude, therefore, will be a cognitive one, for example, a belief. (I use 'utterance' as a neutral word to apply to any candidate for meaning$_{NN}$; it has a convenient act-object ambiguity.) It is no doubt the case that many people have a tendency to put on a tail coat when they think they are about to go to a dance, and it is no doubt also the case that many people, on seeing someone put on a tail coat, would conclude that the person in question was about to go to a dance. Does this satisfy us that putting on a tail coat means$_{NN}$ that one is

---

[1] *Ethics and Language* (New Haven, 1944), ch. iii.

[2] Ibid., p. 57.

about to go to a dance (or indeed means$_{NN}$ anything at all)? Obviously not. It is no help to refer to the qualifying phrase 'dependent on an elaborate process of conditioning . . .'. For if all this means is that the response to the sight of a tail coat being put on is in some way learned or acquired, it will not exclude the present case from being one of meaning$_{NN}$. But if we have to take seriously the second part of the qualifying phrase ('attending the use of the sign in communication'), then the account of meaning$_{NN}$ is obviously circular. We might just as well say, 'X has meaning$_{NN}$ if it is used in communication', which, though true, is not helpful.

(2) If this is not enough, there is a difficulty—really the same difficulty, I think—which Stevenson recognizes: how we are to avoid saying, for example, that 'Jones is tall' is part of what is meant by 'Jones is an athlete', since to tell someone that Jones is an athlete would tend to make him believe that Jones is tall. Stevenson here resorts to invoking linguistic rules, namely, a permissive rule of language that 'athletes may be non-tall'. This amounts to saying that we are not prohibited by rule from speaking of 'non-tall athletes'. But why are we not prohibited? Not because it is not bad grammar, or is not impolite, and so on, but presumably because it is not meaningless (or, if this is too strong, does not in any way violate the rules of meaning for the expressions concerned). But this seems to involve us in another circle. Moreover, one wants to ask why, if it is legitimate to appeal here to rules to distinguish what is meant from what is suggested, this appeal was not made earlier, in the case of groans, for example, to deal with which Stevenson originally introduced the qualifying phrase about dependence on conditioning.

A further deficiency in a causal theory of the type just expounded seems to be that, even if we accept it as it stands, we are furnished with an analysis only of statements about the *standard* meaning, or the meaning in general, of a 'sign'. No provision is made for dealing with statements about what a particular speaker or writer means by a sign on a particular occasion (which may well diverge from the standard meaning of the sign); nor is it obvious how the theory could be adapted to make such provision. One might even go further in criticism and maintain that the causal theory ignores the fact that the meaning (in general) of a sign needs to be explained in terms of what users of the sign do (or should) mean by it on particular occasions; and so the latter notion, which is unexplained by the causal theory, is in fact the fundamental one. I am sympathetic to this more radical criticism, though I am aware that the point is controversial.

I do not propose to consider any further theories of the 'causal-tendency' type. I suspect no such theory could avoid difficulties analogous to those I have outlined without utterly losing its claim to rank as a theory of this type.

I will now try a different and, I hope, more promising line. If we can elucidate the meaning of

'x meant$_{NN}$ something (on a particular occasion)' and
'x meant$_{NN}$ that so-and-so (on a particular occasion)'

and of

'A meant$_{NN}$ something by x (on a particular occasion)' and
'A meant$_{NN}$ by x that so-and-so (on a particular occasion)',

this might reasonably be expected to help us with

'x means$_{NN}$ (timeless) something (that so-and-so)',
'A means$_{NN}$ (timeless) by x something (that so-and-so)',

and with the explication of 'means the same as', 'understands', 'entails', and so on. Let us for the moment pretend that we have to deal only with utterances which might be informative or descriptive.

A first shot would be to suggest that 'x meant$_{NN}$ something' would be true if x was intended by its utterer to induce a belief in some 'audience' and that to say what the belief was would be to say what x meant$_{NN}$. This will not do. I might leave B's handkerchief near the scene of a murder in order to induce the detective to believe that B was the murderer; but we should not want to say that the handkerchief (or my leaving it there) meant$_{NN}$ anything or that I had meant$_{NN}$ by leaving it that B was the murderer. Clearly we must at least add that, for x to have meant$_{NN}$ anything, not merely must it have been 'uttered' with the intention of inducing a certain belief but also the utterer must have intended an 'audience' to recognize the intention behind the utterance.

This, though perhaps better, is not good enough. Consider the following cases:

(1) Herod presents Salome with the head of St. John the Baptist on a charger.

(2) Feeling faint, a child lets its mother see how pale it is (hoping that she may draw her own conclusions and help).

(3) I leave the china my daughter has broken lying around for my wife to see.

Here we seem to have cases which satisfy the conditions so far given for meaning$_{NN}$. For example, Herod intended to make Salome believe that St. John the Baptist was dead and no doubt also intended Salome to recognize that he intended her to believe that St. John the Baptist was dead. Similarly for the other cases. Yet I certainly do not think that we should want to say that we have here cases of meaning$_{NN}$.

What we want to find is the difference between, for example, 'deliberately and openly letting someone know' and 'telling' and between 'getting someone to think' and 'telling'.

The way out is perhaps as follows. Compare the following two cases:

(1) I show Mr. *X* a photograph of Mr. *Y* displaying undue familiarity to Mrs. *X*.

(2) I draw a picture of Mr. *Y* behaving in this manner and show it to Mr. *X*.

I find that I want to deny that in (1) the photograph (or my showing it to Mr. *X*) mean$_{NN}$ anything at all; while I want to assert that in (2) the picture (or my drawing and showing it) meant$_{NN}$ something (that Mr. *Y* had been unduly unfamiliar), or at least that I had meant$_{NN}$ by it that Mr. *Y* had been unduly familiar. What is the difference between the two cases? Surely that in case (1) Mr. *X*'s recognition of my intention to make him believe that there is something between Mr. *Y* and Mrs. *X* is (more or less) irrelevant to the production of this effect by the photograph. Mr. *X* would be led by the photograph at least to suspect Mrs. *X* even if instead of showing it to him I had left it in his room by accident; and I (the photograph shower) would not be unaware of this. But it will make a difference to the effect of my picture on Mr. *X* whether or not he takes me to be intending to inform him (make him believe something) about Mrs. *X*, and not to be just doodling or trying to produce a work of art.

But now we seem to be landed in a further difficulty if we accept this account. For consider now, say, frowning. If I frown spontaneously, in the ordinary course of events, someone looking at me may well treat the frown as a natural sign of displeasure. But if I frown deliberately (to convey my displeasure), an onlooker may be expected, provided he recognizes my intention, *still* to conclude that I am displeased. Ought we not then to say, since it could not be expected to make any difference to the onlooker's reaction whether he regards my frown as spontaneous or as intended to be informative, that my frown (deliberate) does *not* mean$_{NN}$ anything? I think this difficulty can be met; for though in general a deliberate frown may have the same effect (as regards inducing belief in my displeasure) as a spontaneous frown, it can be expected to have the same effect only *provided* the audience takes it as intended to convey displeasure. That is, if we take away the recognition of intention, leaving the other circumstances (including the recognition of the frown as deliberate), the belief-producing tendency of the frown must be regarded as being impaired or destroyed.

Perhaps we may sum up what is necessary for *A* to mean something by *x* as follows. *A* must intend to induce by *x* a belief in an audience, and he must also intend his utterance to be recognized as so intended. But these intentions are not independent; the recognition is intended by *A* to play its part in inducing the belief, and if it does not do so something will have gone wrong with the fulfilment of *A*'s intentions. Moreover, *A*'s intending that the recognition should play this part implies, I think, that he assumes that there is some chance that it will in fact play this part, that he does not regard it as a foregone conclusion that the belief will be induced in the audience whether or not the intention behind the utterance is recognized. Shortly, perhaps, we may say that '*A* meant something by *x*' is roughly equivalent to '*A* uttered *x* with the intention of inducing a belief by means of the recognition of this intention'. (This seems to involve a reflexive paradox, but it does not really do so.)

Now perhaps it is time to drop the pretence that we have to deal only with 'informative' cases. Let us start with some examples of imperatives or quasi-imperatives. I have a very avaricious man in my room, and I want him to go; so I throw a pound note out of the window. Is there here any utterance with a meaning? No, because in behaving as I did, I did not intend his recognition of my purpose to be in any way effective in getting him to go. This is parallel to the photograph case. If on the other hand I had pointed to the door or given him a little push, then my behaviour might well be held to constitute a meaningful utterance, just because the recognition of my intention would be intended by me to be effective in speeding his departure. Another pair of cases would be (1) a policeman who stops a car by standing in its way and (2) a policeman who stops a car by waving.

Or, to turn briefly to another type of case, if as an examiner I fail a man, I may well cause him distress or indignation or humiliation; and if I am vindictive, I may intend this effect and even intend him to recognize my intention. But I should not be inclined to say that my failing him meant anything. On the other hand, if I cut someone in the street I do feel inclined to assimilate this to the cases of meaning, and this inclination seems to me dependent on the fact that I could not reasonably expect him to be distressed (indignant, humiliated) unless he recognized my intention to affect him in this way. (Cf., if my college stopped my salary altogether I should accuse them of ruining me; if they cut it by 2s. 6d I might accuse them of insulting me; with some intermediate amounts I might not know quite what to say.)

Perhaps then we may make the following generalizations.

(1) 'A meant something by x' is (roughly) equivalent to 'A intended the utterance of x to produce some effect in an audience by means of the recognition of this intention'; and we may add that to ask what A meant is to ask for a specification of the intended effect (though, of course, it may not always be possible to get a straight answer involving a 'that' clause, for example, 'a belief that . . .').

(2) 'x meant something' is (roughly) equivalent to 'Somebody meant something by x'. Here again there will be cases where this will not quite work. I feel inclined to say that (as regards traffic lights) the change to red meant that the traffic was to stop; but it would be very unnatural to say, 'Somebody (e.g., the Corporation) meant by the red-light change that the traffic was to stop.' Nevertheless, there seems to be *some* sort of reference to somebody's intentions.

(3) 'x means$_{NN}$ (timeless) that so-and-so' might as a first shot be equated with some statement or disjunction of statements about what 'people' (vague) intend (with qualifications about 'recognition') to effect by x. I shall have a word to say about this.

Will any kind of intended effect do, or may there be cases where an effect is intended (with the required qualifications) and yet we should not want to talk of meaning$_{NN}$? Suppose I discovered some person so constituted that, when I told him that whenever I grunted in a special way I wanted him to blush or to incur some physical malady, thereafter whenever he recognized the grunt (and with it my intention), he did blush or incur the malady. Should we then want to say that the grunt meant$_{NN}$ something? I do not think so. This points to the fact that for x to have meaning$_{NN}$, the intended effect must be something which in some sense is within the control of the audience, or that in some sense of 'reason' the recognition of the intention behind x is for the audience a reason and not merely a cause. It might look as if there is a sort of pun here ('reason for believing' and 'reason for doing'), but I do not think this is serious. For though no doubt from one point of view questions about reasons for believing are questions about evidence and so quite different from questions about reasons for doing, nevertheless to recognize an utterer's intention in uttering x (descriptive utterance), to have a reason for believing that so-and-so, is at least quite like 'having a motive for' accepting so-and-so. Decisions 'that' seem to involve decisions 'to' (and this is why we can 'refuse to believe' and also be 'compelled to believe'). (The 'cutting' case needs slightly different treatment, for one cannot in any straightforward sense 'decide' to be offended; but one can refuse to be offended.) It looks then as if the intended effect must be something within the control of the audience, or at least the *sort* of thing which is within its control.

One point before passing to an objection or two. I think it follows that from what I have said about the connexion between meaning$_{NN}$ and recognition of intention that (insofar as I am right) only what I may call the primary intention of an utterer is relevant to the meaning$_{NN}$ of an utterance. For if I utter x, intending (with the aid of the recognition of this intention) to induce an effect E, and intend this effect E to lead to a further effect F, then insofar as the occurrence of F is thought to be dependent solely on E, I cannot regard F as in the least dependent on recognition of my intention to induce E. That is, if (say) I intend to get a man to do something by giving him some information, it cannot be regarded as relevant to the meaning$_{NN}$ of my utterance to describe what I intend him to do.

Now some question may be raised about my use, fairly free, of such words as 'intention' and 'recognition'. I must disclaim any intention of peopling all our talking life with armies of complicated psychological occurrences. I do not hope to solve any philosophical puzzles about intending, but I do want briefly to argue that no special difficulties are raised by my use of the word 'intention' in connexion with meaning. First, there will be cases where an utterance is accompanied or preceded by a conscious 'plan', or explicit formulation of intention (e.g., I declare how I am going to use x, or ask myself how to 'get something across'). The presence of such an explicit 'plan' obviously counts fairly heavily in favour of the utterer's intention (meaning) being as 'planned'; though it is not, I think, conclusive; for example, a speaker who has declared an intention to use a familiar expression in an unfamiliar way may slip into the familiar use. Similarly in non-linguistic cases: if we are asking about an agent's intention, a previous expression counts heavily; nevertheless, a man might plan to throw a letter in the dustbin and yet take it to the post; when lifting his hand he might 'come to' and say *either* 'I didn't intend to do this at all' *or* 'I suppose I must have been intending to put it in'.

Explicitly formulated linguistic (or quasi-linguistic) intentions are no doubt comparatively rare. In their absence we would seem to rely on very much the same kinds of criteria as we do in the case of non-linguistic intentions where there is a general usage. An utterer is held to intend to convey what is normally conveyed (or normally intended to be conveyed), and we require a good reason for accepting that a particular use diverges from the general usage (e.g., he never knew or had forgotten the general usage). Similarly in non-linguistic cases: we are presumed to intend the normal consequences of our actions.

Again, in cases where there is doubt, say, about which of two or more things an utterer intends to convey, we tend to refer to the context (linguistic or otherwise) of the utterance and ask which of the alternatives would be relevant to other things he is saying or doing, or which intention in a particular situation would fit in with some purpose he obviously has (e.g., a man who calls for a 'pump' at a fire would not want a bicycle pump). Non-linguistic parallels are obvious: context is a criterion in settling the question of why a man who has just put a cigarette in his mouth has put his hand in his pocket; relevance to an obvious end is a criterion in settling why a man is running away from a bull.

In certain linguistic cases we ask the utterer afterwards about his intention, and in a few of these cases (the very difficult ones, like a philosopher asked to explain the meaning of an unclear passage in one of his works), the answer is not based on what he remembers but is more like a decision, a decision about how what he said is to be taken. I cannot find a non-linguistic parallel here; but the case is so special as not to seem to contribute a vital difference.

All this is very obvious; but surely to show that the criteria for judging linguistic intentions are very like the criteria for judging non-linguistic intentions is to show that linguistic intentions are very like non-linguistic intentions.

III

TRUTH

MICHAEL DUMMETT

FREGE held that truth and falsity are the references of sentences. Sentences cannot stand for propositions (what Frege calls 'thoughts'), since the reference of a complex expression depends only on the reference of its parts; whereas if we substitute for a singular term occurring in a sentence another singular term with the same reference but a different sense, the sense of the whole sentence, i.e., the thought which it expresses, changes. The only thing which it appears *must* in these circumstances remain unchanged is the truth-value of the sentence. The expressions 'is true' and 'is false' look like predicates applying to propositions, and one might suppose that truth and falsity were properties of propositions; but it now appears that the relation between a proposition and its truth-value is not like that between a table and its shape, but rather like that between the sense of a definite description and the actual object for which it stands.

To the objection that there are non-truth-functional occurrences of sentences as parts of complex sentences, e.g., clauses in indirect speech, Frege replies that in such contexts we must take ordinary singular terms as standing, not for their customary reference, but for their sense, and hence we may say that in such a context, and only then, a sentence stands for the proposition it usually expresses.

If someone asks, 'But what kind of entities are these truth-values supposed to be?' we may reply that there is no more difficulty in seeing what the truth-value of a sentence may be than there is in seeing what the direction of a line may be; we have been told when two sentences have the same truth-value—when they are materially equivalent—just as we know when two lines have the same direction—when they are parallel. Nor need we waste time on the objection raised by Max Black that on Frege's theory certain sentences become meaningful which we should not normally regard as such, e.g., 'If oysters are inedible, then the False'. If sentences stand for truth-values, but there are also expressions standing for truth-values which

From *Proceedings of the Aristotelian Society*, Vol. 59 (1958–9), pp. 141–62. Reprinted by courtesy of the author and the Editor of the Aristotelian Society.

are not sentences, then the objection to allowing expressions of the latter kind to stand wherever sentences can stand and vice versa is grammatical, not logical. We often use the word 'thing' to provide a noun where grammar demands one and we have only an adjective, e.g., in 'That was a disgraceful thing to do'; and we could introduce a verb, say 'trues', to fulfil the purely grammatical function of converting a noun standing for a truth-value into a sentence standing for the same truth-value. It may be said that Frege has proved that a sentence does not ordinarily stand for a proposition, and has given a plausible argument that *if* sentences have references, they stand for truth-values, but that he has done nothing to show that sentences do have references at all. This is incorrect; Frege's demonstration that the notions of a concept (property) and a relation can be explained as special cases of the notion of a function provides a plausible argument for saying that sentences have a reference.

What *is* questionable is Frege's use of the words 'truth' and 'falsity' as names of the references of sentences; for by using these words rather than invented words of his own he gives the impression that by taking sentences to have a reference, with material equivalence as the criterion of identity, he has given an account of the notions of truth and falsity which we are accustomed to employ. Let us compare truth and falsity with the winning and losing of a board game. For a particular game we may imagine first formulating the rules by specifying the initial position and the permissible moves; the game comes to an end when there is no permissible move. We may then distinguish between two (or three) kinds of final positions, which we call 'Win' (meaning that the player to make the first move wins), 'Lose' (similarly), and, possibly, 'Draw'. Unless we tacitly appeal to the usual meanings of the words 'win', 'lose' and 'draw', this description leaves out one vital point—that it is the object of a player to win. It is part of the concept of winning a game that a player plays to win, and this part of the concept is not conveyed by a classification of the end positions into winning ones and losing ones. We can imagine a variant of chess in which it is the object of each player to be checkmated, and this would be an entirely different game; but the formal description we imagined would coincide with the formal description of chess. The whole theory of chess could be formulated with reference only to the formal description; but which theorems of this theory interested us would depend upon whether we wished to play chess or the variant game. Likewise, it is part of the concept of truth that we aim at making true statements; and Frege's theory of truth and falsity as the references of sentences leaves this feature of the concept of truth quite out of account. Frege indeed tried to bring it in afterwards, in his theory of assertion—but too late; for the sense of the sentence is not given in advance of our going in for the activity of asserting, since otherwise there could be people who expressed the same thoughts but went in instead for denying them.

A similar criticism applies to many accounts of truth and falsity or of the meanings of certain sentences in terms of truth and falsity. We cannot in general suppose that we give a proper account of a concept by describing those circumstances in which we do, and those in which we do not, make use of the relevant word, by describing the *usage* of that word; we must also give an account of the *point* of the concept, explain what we use the word *for*. Classifications do not exist in the void, but are connected always with some interest which we have, so that to assign something to one class or another will have consequences connected with this interest. A clear example is the problem of justifying a form of argument, deductive or inductive. Classification of arguments into (deductively or inductively) valid and invalid ones is not a game played merely for its own sake, although it *could* be taught without reference to any purpose or interest, say as a school exercise. Hence there is really a problem of showing that the criteria we employ for recognizing valid arguments do in fact serve the purpose we intend them to serve: the problem is not to be dismissed—as it has long been fashionable to do—by saying that we use the criteria we use.

We cannot assume that a classification effected by means of a predicate in use in a language will always have just *one* point. It may be that the classification of statements into true ones, false ones, and, perhaps, those that are neither true nor false, has one principal point, but that other subsidiary ends are served by it which make the use of the words 'true' and 'false' more complex than it would otherwise be. At one time it was usual to say that we do not call ethical statements 'true' or 'false', and from this many consequences for ethics were held to flow. But the question is not whether these words are in practice applied to ethical statements, but whether, if they were so applied, the point of doing so would be the same as the point of applying them to statements of other kinds, and, if not, in what ways it would be different. Again, to be told that we say of a statement containing a singular term which lacks reference that it is neither true nor false is so far only to be informed of a point of usage; no philosophical consequences can yet be drawn. Rather, we need to ask whether describing such a statement as neither true nor false accords better with the general point of classifying statements as true or false than to describe it as false. Suppose that we learn that in a particular language such statements are described as 'false': how are we to tell whether this shows that they use such statements differently from ourselves or merely that 'false' is not an exact translation of their word? To say that we use singular statements in such a way that they are neither true nor false when the subject has no reference is meant to characterize our use of singular statements; hence it ought to be possible to describe when in a language not containing words for 'true' and 'false' singular statements would be used in the same way as we use them, and when they would be used so as to be false when the subject had no reference. Until we have an account of the general point of the classification into true and false we do not know what interest attaches to saying of certain statements that they are neither true nor false; and until we have an account of how the truth-conditions of a statement determine its meaning the description of the meaning by stating the truth conditions is valueless.

A popular account of the meaning of the word 'true', also deriving from Frege, is that ⌜It is true that P⌝ has the same sense as the sentence P. If we then ask why it is any use to have the word 'true' in the language, the answer is that we often refer to propositions indirectly, i.e., without expressing them, as when we say 'Goldbach's conjecture' or 'what the witness said'. We also generalize about propositions without referring to any particular one, e.g., in 'Everything he says is true'. This explanation cannot rank as a definition in the strict sense, since it permits elimination of 'is true' only when it occurs attached to a that-clause, and not when attached to any other expression standing for a proposition or to a variable; but, since every proposition can be expressed by a sentence, this does not refute its claim to be considered as determining uniquely the sense of 'is true'. It might be compared with the recursive definition of '+', which enables us to eliminate the sign '+' only when it occurs in front of a numeral, and not when it occurs in front of any other expression for a number or in front of a variable; yet there is a clear mathematical sense in which it specifies uniquely what operation '+' is to signify. Similarly, our explanation of 'is true' determines uniquely the sense, or at least the application, of this predicate: for any given proposition there is a sentence expressing that proposition, and that sentence states the conditions under which the proposition is true.

If, as Frege thought, there exist sentences which express propositions but are neither true nor false, then this explanation appears incorrect. Suppose that P contains a singular term which has a sense but no reference: then, according to Frege, P expresses a proposition which has no truth-value. This proposition is therefore not true, and hence the statement ⌜It is true that P⌝ will be *false*. P will therefore not have the same sense as ⌜It is true that P⌝, since the latter is false while the former is not. It is not possible to plead that ⌜It is true that P⌝ is itself neither true nor false when the singular term occurring in P lacks a reference, since the *oratio obliqua* clause ⌜that P⌝ stands for the proposition expressed by P, and it is admitted that P does have a sense and express a proposition; the singular term occurring in P has in ⌜It is true that P⌝ its indirect reference, namely its sense, and we assumed that it did have a sense. In general, it will always be inconsistent to maintain the truth of every instance of 'It is true that p if and only if p' while allowing that there is a type of sentence which under certain conditions is neither true nor false. It would be possible to evade this objection by claiming that the 'that'-clause in a sentence beginning 'It is true that' is not an instance of *oratio obliqua*; that the word 'that' here serves the purely grammatical function of transforming a sentence into a noun-clause without altering either its sense or its reference. We should then have to take phrases like 'Goldbach's conjecture' and 'what the witness said' as standing not for propositions but for truth-values. The expression 'is true' would then be exactly like the verb 'trues' which we imagined earlier; it would simply convert a noun-phrase standing for a truth-value into a sentence without altering its sense or its reference. It might be objected that this variant of Frege's account tallies badly with his saying that it is the *thought* (proposition) which is what is true or false; but we can express this point of Frege's by saying that it is the *thought*, rather than the *sentence*, which primarily stands for a truth-value. A stronger objection to the variant account is that it leans heavily on the theory of truth-values as references of sentences, while the original version depends only on the more plausible view that clauses in indirect speech stand for propositions. In any case, if there are meaningful sentences which say nothing which is true or false, then there must be *a* use of the word 'true' which applies to propositions; for if we say ⌜It is neither true nor false that P⌝, the clause ⌜that P⌝ must here be in *oratio obliqua*, otherwise the whole sentence would lack a truth-value.

Even if we do not wish to say of certain statements that they are neither true nor false, this account cannot give the *whole* meaning of the word 'true'. If we are to give an explanation of the word 'false' parallel to our explanation of 'true' we shall have to say that ⌜It is false that P⌝ has the same sense as the negation of P. In logical symbolism there exists a sign which, put in front of a sentence, forms the negation of that sentence; but in natural languages we do not have such a sign. We have to think to realize that the negation of 'No-one is here' is not 'No-one is not here' but 'Some-one is here'; there is no one rule for forming the negation of a given sentence. Now according to what principle do we recognize one sentence as the negation of another? It is natural to answer: The negation of a sentence P is that sentence which is true if and only if P is false and false if and only if P is true. But this explanation is ruled out if we want to use the notion of the negation of a sentence in order to explain the sense of the word 'false'. It would not solve the difficulty if we did have a general sign of negation analogous to the logical symbol, for the question would then be: How in general do we determine the sense of the negation, given the sense of the original sentence?

We encounter the same difficulty over the connective 'or'. We can give an account of the meaning of 'and' by saying that we are in a position to assert ⌜P and Q⌝ when and only when we are in a position to assert P and in a position to assert Q. (This is not circular: one could train a dog to bark only when a bell rang *and* a light shone without presupposing that it possessed the concept of conjunction.) But, if we accept a two-valued logic, we cannot give a similar explanation of the meaning of 'or'. We often assert ⌜P or Q⌝ when we are not either in a position to assert P or in a position to assert Q. I use the word 'we' here, meaning mankind, advisedly. If the history master gives the schoolboy a hint, saying, 'It was either James I or Charles I who was beheaded', then the schoolboy is in a position to assert, 'Either James I or Charles I was beheaded' without (perhaps) being in a position to assert either limb of the disjunction; but it is not this sort of case which causes the difficulty. The *ultimate* source of the schoolboy's knowledge derives from something which justifies the assertion that Charles I was beheaded; and this is all that would be required for the proposed explanation of the word 'or' to be adequate. Likewise, the explanation is not impugned by cases like that in which I remember that I was talking either to Jean or to Alice, but cannot remember which. My knowledge that I was talking either to Jean or to Alice derives ultimately from the knowledge that I had at the time that I was talking to (say) Jean; the fact that the incomplete knowledge is all that survives is beside the point. Rather, the difficulty arises because we often make statements of the form ⌜P or Q⌝ when the ultimate evidence for making them, in the sense indicated, is neither evidence for the truth of P nor evidence for the truth of Q. The most striking instance of this is the fact that we are prepared to assert *any* statement of the form ⌜P or not P⌝, even though we may have no evidence either for the truth of P or for the truth of ⌜Not P⌝.

In order to justify asserting ⌜P or not P⌝, we appeal to the truth-table explanation of the meaning of 'or'. But if the whole explanation of the meanings of 'true' and 'false' is given by 'It is true that p if and only if p' and 'It is false that p if and only if not p', this appeal fails. The truth-table tells us, e.g., that from P we may infer ⌜P or Q⌝ (in particular, ⌜P or not P⌝); but *that* much we already knew from the explanation of 'or' which we have rejected as insufficient. The truth-table does not show us that we are entitled to assert ⌜P or not P⌝ in every possible case, since this is to assume that every statement is either true or false; but, if our explanation of 'true' and 'false' is all the explanation that can be given, to say that every statement is either true or false is just to say that we are always justified in saying ⌜P or not P⌝.

We naturally think of truth-tables as giving the explanation of the sense which we attach to the sign of negation and to the connectives, an explanation which will show that we are justified in regarding certain forms of statement as logically true. It now appears that if we accept the redundancy theory of 'true' and 'false'—the theory that our explanation gives the whole meaning of these words—the truth-table explanation is quite unsatisfactory. More generally, we must abandon the idea which we naturally have that the notions of truth and falsity play an essential role in any account either of the meaning of statements in general or of the meaning of a particular statement. The conception pervades the thought of Frege that the general form of explanation of the sense of a statement consists in laying down the conditions under which it is true and those under which it is false (or better: saying that it is false under all other conditions); this same conception is expressed in the *Tractatus* in the words, 'In order to be able to say that "p" is true (or false), I must have determined under what conditions I call "p" true, and this is how I determine the sense of the sentence' (4.063). But in order that someone should gain from the explanation that P is true in such-and-such circumstances an understanding of the sense of P, he must already know what it means to say of P that it is true. If when he inquires into this he is told that the only explanation is that to say that P is true is the same as to assert P, it will follow that in order to understand what is meant by saying that P is true, he must already know the sense of asserting P, which was precisely what was supposed to be being explained to him.

We thus have either to supplement the redundancy theory or to give up many of our preconceptions about truth and falsity. It has become a commonplace to say that there cannot be a criterion of truth. The argument is that we determine the sense of a sentence by laying down the conditions under which it is true, so that we could not first know the sense of a sentence and then apply some criterion to decide in what circumstances it was true. In the same sense there could not be a criterion for what constitutes the winning of a game, since learning what constitutes winning it is an essential part of learning what the game is. This does not mean that there may not be in any sense a theory of truth. For a particular bounded language, if it is free of ambiguity and inconsistency, it must be possible to characterize the true sentences of the language; somewhat as, for a given game, we can say which moves are winning moves. (A language is bounded if we may not introduce into it new words or new senses for old words.) Such a characterization would be recursive, defining truth first for the simplest possible sentences, and then for sentences built out of others by the logical operations employed in the language; this is what is done for formalized languages by a truth-definition. The redundancy theory gives the general form of such a truth-definition, though in particular cases more informative definitions might be given.

Now we have seen that to say for each particular game what winning it consists in is not to give a satisfactory account of the concept of winning a game. What makes us use the same term 'winning' for each of these various activities is that the point of every game is that each player tries to do what for that game constitutes winning; i.e., what constitutes winning always plays the same part in determining what playing the game consists in. Similarly, what the truth of a statement consists in always plays the same role in determining the sense of that statement, and a theory of truth must be possible in the sense of an account of what that role is. I shall not now attempt such an account; I claim, however, that such an account would justify the following. A statement, so long as it is not ambiguous or vague, divides all possible states of affairs into just *two* classes. For a given state of affairs, either the statement is used in such a way that a man who asserted it but envisaged that state of affairs as a possibility would be held to have spoken misleadingly, or the assertion of the statement would not be taken as expressing the speaker's exclusion of that possibility. If a state of affairs of the first kind obtains, the statement is false; if all actual states of affairs are of the second kind, it is true. It is thus prima facie senseless to say of any statement that in such-and-such a state of affairs would be neither true nor false.

The sense of a statement is determined by knowing in what circumstances it is true and in what false. Likewise the sense of a command is determined by knowing what constitutes obedience to it and what disobedience; and the sense of a bet by knowing when the bet is won and when it is lost. Now there may be a gap between the winning of a bet and the losing of it, as with a conditional bet; can there be a similar gap between obedience and disobedience to a command, or between the truth and falsity of a statement? There is a distinction between a conditional bet and a bet on the truth of a material conditional; if the antecedent is unfulfilled, in the first case the bet is off—it is just as if no bet had been made—but in the second case the bet is won. A conditional command where the antecedent is in the power of the person given the order (e.g., a mother says to a child, 'If you go out, wear your coat') is always like a bet on the material conditional; it is equivalent to the command to ensure the truth of the material conditional, viz., 'Do not go out without your coat.' We cannot say that if the child does not go out, it is just as if no command had been given, since it may be that, unable to find his coat, he stayed in in order to comply with the command.

Can a distinction parallel to that for bets be drawn for conditional commands where the antecedent is not in the person's power? I contend that the distinction which looks as if it could be drawn is in fact void of significance. There are two distinct kinds of consequence of making a bet, winning it and losing; to determine what is to involve one of these is not yet to determine completely what is to involve the other. But there is only one kind of consequence of giving a command, namely that, provided one had the right to give it in the first place, one acquires a right to punish or at least reprobate disobedience. It might be thought that punishment and reward were distinct consequences of a command in the same sense that paying money and receiving it are distinct consequences of a bet; but this does not tally with the role of commands in our society. The right to a reward is not taken to be an automatic consequence of obedience to a command, as the *right* to reproach is an automatic consequence of disobedience; if a reward is given, this is an act of grace, just as it is an act of grace if the punishment or reproach is withheld. Moreover, any action deliberately taken in order to comply with the command (to avoid disobedience to it) has the same claim to be rewarded as any other; hence to determine what constitutes disobedience to the command is thereby to determine what sort of behaviour might be rewarded, without the need for any further decision. If the child stays in because he cannot find his coat, this behaviour is as meritorious as if he goes out remembering to wear it; and if he forgets all about the order, but wears his coat for some other reason, this behaviour no more deserves commendation than if he chooses, for selfish reasons, to remain indoors. Where the antecedent is not in the person's power, it is indeed possible to regard the conditional command as analogous to the conditional bet; but since obedience to a command has no consequence of its own other than that of avoiding the punishment due for disobedience, there is not for such commands any significant distinction parallel to that between conditional bets and bets about a material conditional. If we regarded obedience to a command as giving a right to a reward, we could then introduce such a distinction for commands whose antecedent was in the person's power. Thus the mother might use the form, 'If you go out, wear your coat', as involving that if the child went out with his coat he would be rewarded, if he went out without it he would be punished, and if he stayed indoors—even in order to comply with the command—he would be neither punished nor rewarded; while the form, 'Do not go out without your coat', would involve his being rewarded if he stayed indoors.

Statements are like commands (as we use them) and not like bets; the making of a statement has, as it were, only one kind of consequence. To see this, let us imagine a language which contains conditional statements but has no counterfactual form (counterfactuals would introduce irrelevant complications). Two alternative accounts are suggested of the way in which conditionals are used in this language: one, that they are used to make statements conditionally; the other, that they represent the material conditional. On the first interpretation, a conditional statement is like a conditional bet: if the antecedent is fulfilled, then the statement is treated as if it had been an unconditional assertion of the consequent, and is said to be true or false accordingly; if the antecedent is not fulfilled, then it is just as if no statement, true or false, had been made at all. On the second interpretation, if the antecedent is not fulfilled, then the statement is said to be true. How are we to settle which of these two accounts is the correct one? If statements are really like bets and not like commands; if there are two distinct kinds of consequence which may follow the making of a statement, those that go with calling the statement 'true' and those that go with calling it 'false', so that there may be a gap between these two kinds of consequence; then we ought to be able to find something which decides between the two accounts as definite as the financial transaction which distinguishes a bet on the truth of the material conditional from a conditional bet. It is no use asking whether these people *say* that the man who has made a conditional statement whose antecedent turns out false said something true or that he said nothing true or false: they may have no words corresponding to 'true' and 'false'; and if they do, how could we be sure that the correspondence was exact? If their using the words 'true' and 'false' is to have the slightest significance, there must be some difference in their behaviour which goes with their saying 'true' or 'neither true nor false' in this case.

It is evident on reflection that there is nothing in what they do which could distinguish between the two alternative accounts; the distinction between them is as empty as the analogous distinction for conditional commands whose antecedent is not in the person's power. In order to fix the sense of an utterance, we do not need to make two separate decisions—when to say that a true statement has been made and when to say that a false statement has been made; rather, any situation in which nothing obtains which is taken as a case of its being false may be regarded as a case of its being true, just as someone who behaves so as not to disobey a command may be regarded as having obeyed it. The point becomes clearer when we look at it in the following way. If it makes sense in general to suppose that a certain form of statement is so used that in certain circumstances it is true, in others false, and in yet others nothing has been said true or false, then we can imagine that a form of conditional was used in this way (von Wright actually holds that *we* use conditionals in this way). If P turns out true, then ⌜If P, then Q⌝ is said to be true or false according as Q is true or false, while if P turns out false we say that nothing was said true or false. Let us contrast this with what Frege and Strawson say about the use in our language of statements containing a singular term. If there is an object for which the singular term stands, then the statement is true or false according as the predicate does or does not apply to that object, but if there is no such object, then we have not said anything true or false. Now do these accounts tell us the sense of sentences of these two kinds?—that is, do they tell us how these statements are used, what is *done* by making statements of these forms? Not at all, for an essential feature of their use has not yet been laid down. Someone uttering a conditional statement of the kind described may very well have no opinion as to whether the antecedent was going to turn out true or false; that is, he is not taken as having misused the statement or misled his hearers if he envisages it as a possibility that that case will arise in which he is said not to have made a statement true or false. All that he conveys by uttering the conditional statement is that he excludes the possibility that the case will arise in which he is said to have said something false, namely that antecedent is true and consequent false. With the case of a singular statement it is quite different. Here someone is definitely either misusing the form of statement or misleading his hearers if he envisages it as a possibility that that case will arise in which what he said will be said to be neither true nor false, namely that the singular term has no reference. He conveys more by making the statement than just that he excludes the possibility of its being false; he commits himself to its being true.

Are we then to say that laying down the truth-conditions for a sentence is not sufficient to determine its sense, that something further will have to be stipulated as well? Rather than say this we should abandon the notions of truth and falsity altogether. In order to characterize the sense of expressions of our two forms, only a twofold classification of possible relevant circumstances is necessary. We need to distinguish those states of affairs such that if the speaker envisaged them as possibilities he would be held to be either misusing the statement or misleading his hearers, and those of which this is not the case: and *one* way of using the words 'true' and 'false' would be to call states of affairs of the former kind those in which the statement was false and the others those in which the statement was true. For our conditional statements, the distinction would be between those states of affairs in which the statement was said to be false and those in which we said that it would either be true or else neither true nor false. For singular statements, the distinction would be between those states of affairs in which we said that the statement would either be false or else neither true nor false, and those in which it was true. To grasp the sense or use of these forms of statement, the twofold classification is quite sufficient; the threefold classification with which we started is entirely beside the point. Thus, on *one* way of using the words 'true' and 'false', we should, instead of distinguishing between the conditional statement's being true and its being neither true nor false, have distinguished between two different ways in which it could be true; and instead of distinguishing between the singular statement's being false and its being neither true nor false, we should have distinguished between two different ways in which it could be false.

This gives us a hint at a way of explaining the role played by truth and falsity in determining the sense of a statement. We have not yet seen what point there may be in distinguishing between different ways in which a statement may be true or between different ways in which it may be false, or, as we might say, between degrees of truth and falsity. The point of such distinctions does not lie in anything to do with the sense of the statement itself, but has to do with the way in which it enters into complex statements. Let us imagine that in the language of which the conditional statements we considered form a part there exists a sign of negation, i.e., a word which, placed in front of a statement, forms another statement; I call it a sign of negation because in most cases it forms a statement which we should regard as being used as the contradictory of the original statement. Let us suppose, however, that when placed in front of a conditional statement ⌜If P, then Q⌝, it forms a statement which is used in the same way as the statement ⌜If P, then not Q⌝. Then if we describe the use of the conditionals by reference to a twofold classification only, i.e., in the same way as we describe a material conditional, we shall be unable to give a truth-functional account of the behaviour of their sign 'not'. That is, we should have the tables:

P	Q	⌜If P, then Q⌝	⌜Not: if P, then Q⌝
T	T	T	F
T	F	F	T
F	T	T	T
F	F	T	T

in which the truth-value of ⌜Not: if P, then Q⌝ is not determined by the truth-value of ⌜If P, then Q⌝. If, on the other hand, we revert to our original threefold classification, marking the case in which we said that no statement true or false had been made by 'X', then we have the tables:

P	Q	⌜If P, then Q⌝	⌜Not: if P, then Q⌝
T	T	T	F
T	F	F	T
F	T	X	X
F	F	X	X

which can be quite satisfactorily accounted for by giving the table for 'not':

R	⌜Not R⌝
T	F
X	X
F	T

(I have assumed that the statements P and Q take only the values T and F). It now becomes quite natural to think of 'T' as representing 'true', 'F' 'false' and 'X' 'neither true nor false'. Then we can say that their symbol 'not' really is a sign of negation, since ⌜Not P⌝ is true when and only when P is false and false when and only when P is true. We must not forget, however, that the justification for distinguishing between the cases in which a conditional was said to have the value T and the cases in which it was said to have the value X was simply the possibility, created by this distinction, of treating 'not' truth-functionally. In the same way if we have in a language an expression which normally functions as a sign of negation, but the effect of prefacing a singular statement with this expression is to produce a statement whose utterance still commits the speaker to there being an object for which the singular term stands, it is very natural to distinguish between two kinds of falsity a singular statement may have: that when the singular term has a reference, but the predicate does not apply to it, and that when the singular term lacks a reference. Let us represent the case in which the singular term has no reference by the symbol 'Y', and let us suppose S to be a singular statement. Then we have the table:

S	⌜Not S⌝
T	F
Y	Y
F	T

Here again it is natural to think of 'T' as representing 'true', 'F' 'false' and 'Y' 'neither true nor false'.

There is no necessity to use the words 'true' and 'false' as suggested above, so that we have to interpret X as a kind of truth and Y as a kind of falsity. Logicians who study many-valued logics have a term which can be employed here: they would say that T and X are 'designated' truth-values and F and Y 'undesignated' ones. (In a many-valued logic those formulas are considered valid which have a designated value for every assignment of values to their sentence-letters.) The points to observe are just these: (i) The sense of a sentence is determined wholly by knowing the case in which it has a designated value and the cases in which it has an undesignated one. (ii) Finer distinctions between different designated values or different undesignated ones, however naturally they come to us, are justified only if they are needed in order to give a truth-functional account of the formation of complex statements by means of operators. (iii) In *most* philosophical discussions of truth and falsity, what we really have in mind is the distinction between a designated and an undesignated value, and hence choosing the names 'truth' and 'falsity' for particular designated and undesignated values respectively will only obscure the issue. (iv) Saying that in certain circumstances a statement is neither true nor false does not determine whether the statement is in that case to count as having an undesignated or a designated value, i.e., whether someone who asserts the statement is or is not taken as excluding the possibility that that case obtains.

Baffled by the attempt to describe in general the relation between language and reality, we have nowadays abandoned the correspondence theory of truth, and justify our doing so on the score that it was an attempt to state a *criterion* of truth in the sense in which this cannot be done. Nevertheless, the correspondence theory expresses one important feature of the concept of truth which is not expressed by the law 'It is true that p if and only if p' and which we have so far left quite out of account: that a statement is true only if there is something in the world *in virtue of which* it is true. Although we no longer accept the correspondence theory, we remain realists *au fond*; we retain in our thinking a fundamentally realist conception of truth. Realism consists in the belief that for any statement there must be something in virtue of which either it or its negation is true: it is only on the basis of this belief that we can justify the idea that truth and falsity play an essential role in the notion of the meaning of a statement, that the general form of an explanation of meaning is a statement of the truth-conditions.

To see the importance of this feature of the concept of truth, let us envisage a dispute over the logical validity of the statement 'Either Jones was brave or he was not'. A imagines Jones to be a man, now dead, who never encountered danger in his life. B retorts that it could still be true that Jones was brave, namely, if it is true that if Jones *had* encountered danger, he would have acted bravely. A agrees with this, but still maintains that it does not need to be the case that either 'Jones was brave' = 'If Jones had encountered danger, he would have acted bravely' nor 'Jones was not brave' = 'If Jones had encountered danger, he would not have acted bravely' is true. For, he argues, it might be the case that however many facts we knew of the kind which we should normally regard as grounds for asserting such counter-factual conditionals, we should still know nothing which would be a ground for asserting either. It is clear that B cannot agree that this is a possibility and yet continue to insist that all the same either 'Jones was brave' or 'Jones was not brave' is true; for he would then be committed to holding that a statement may be true even though there is nothing whatever such that, if we knew of it, we should count it as evidence or as a ground for the truth of the statement, and this is absurd. (It may be objected that there are assertions for which it would be out of place to ask one who made them for his evidence or grounds; but for *such* assertions the speaker must always either be in a position to make or in a position to deny them.) If B still wishes to maintain the necessity of 'Either Jones was brave or he was not', he will have to hold either that there must be some fact of the sort to which we usually appeal in discussing counterfactuals which, if we knew it, would decide us in favour either of the one counterfactual or of the other; or else that there is some fact of extraordinary kind, perhaps known only to God. In the latter case he imagines a kind of spiritual mechanism—Jones' character—which determines how he acts in each situation that arises; his acting in such-and-such a way reveals to us the state of this spiritual mechanism, which was however already in place before its observable effects were displayed in his behaviour. B would then argue thus: If Jones *had* encountered danger, he would either have acted bravely or have acted like a coward. Suppose he had acted bravely. This would then have shown us that he was brave; but he would *already* have been brave before his courage was revealed by his behaviour. That is, either his character included the quality of courage or it did not, and his character determines his behaviour. We know his character only indirectly, through its effects on his behaviour; but each character-trait must be *there* within him independently of whether it reveals itself to us or not.

Anyone of a sufficient degree of sophistication will reject B's belief in a spiritual mechanism; either he will be a materialist and substitute for it an equally blind belief in a physiological mechanism, or he will accept A's conclusion that 'Either Jones was brave or he was not' is not logically necessary. His ground for rejecting B's argument is that if such a statement as 'Jones was brave' is true, it must be true in virtue of the sort of fact we have been taught to regard as justifying us in asserting it. It cannot be true in virtue of a fact of some quite different sort of which we can have no direct knowledge, for otherwise the statement 'Jones was brave' would not have the meaning that *we* have given it. In accepting A's position he makes a small retreat from realism; he abandons a realist view of character.

In order, then, to decide whether a realist account of truth can be given for statements of some particular kind, we have to ask whether for such a statement P it must be the case that if we knew sufficiently many facts of the kind we normally treat as justifying us in asserting P, we should be in a position either to assert P or to assert ⌐Not P⌐: is so, then it can truly be said that there must either be something in virtue of which P is true or something in virtue of which it is false. It is easy to overlook the force of the phrase 'sufficiently many'. Consider the statement 'A city will never be built on this spot'. Even if we have an oracle which can answer every question of the kind, 'Will there be a city here in 1990?' 'In 2100?' etc., we might never be in a position either to declare the statement true or to declare it false. Someone may say: That is only because you are assuming the knowledge of only finitely many answers of the oracle; but if you knew the oracle's answers to *all* these questions, you would be able to decide the truth-value of the statement. But what would it mean to know infinitely many facts? It could mean that the oracle gave a direct answer 'No' to the question, 'Will a city ever be built here?': but to assume this is just like B's assumption of the existence of a hidden spiritual mechanism. It might mean that we had an argument to show the falsity of ⌐A city will be built here in the year N irrespective of the value of N, e.g., if 'here' is the North Pole: but no one would suggest that it must be the case that either the oracle will give an affirmative answer to some question of the form 'Will there be a city here in the year . . . ?' or we can find a general argument for a negative answer. Finally, it could mean that we were *able* to answer every question of the form, 'Will there be a city here in the year . . . ?': but having infinite knowledge in *this* sense will place us in no better position than when we had the oracle.

We thus arrive at the following position. We are entitled to say that a statement P must be either true or false, that there must be something in virtue of which either it is true or it is false, only when P is a statement of such a kind that we could in a finite time bring ourselves into a position in which we were justified either in asserting or in denying P; that is, when P is an effectively decidable statement. This limitation is not trivial: there is an immense range of statements which, like 'Jones was brave', are concealed conditionals, or which, like 'A city will never be built here', contain—explicitly or implicitly—an unlimited generality, and which therefore fail the test.

What I have done here is to transfer to ordinary statements what the intuitionists say about mathematical statements. The sense of e.g., the existential quantifier is determined by considering what sort of fact makes an existential statement true, and this means: the sort of fact which we have been taught to regard as justifying us in asserting an existential statement. What would make the statement that there exists an odd perfect number true would be some particular number's being both odd and perfect; hence the assertion of the existential statement must be taken as a claim to be able to assert some one of the singular statements. We are thus justified in asserting that there is a number with a certain property only if we have a method for finding a particular number with that property. Likewise, the sense of a universal statement is given by the sort of consideration we regard as justifying us in asserting it: namely we can assert that every number has a certain property if we have a general method for showing, for any arbitrary number, that it has that property. Now what if someone insists that either the statement 'There is an odd perfect number' is true, or else every perfect number is even? He is justified if he knows of a procedure which will lead him in a finite time either to the determination of a particular odd perfect number or to a general proof that a number assumed to be perfect is even. But if he knows of no such procedure, then he is trying to attach to the statement 'Every perfect number is even' a meaning which lies *beyond* that provided by the training we are given in the use of universal statements; he wants to say, as B said of 'Jones was brave', that its truth may lie in a region directly accessible only to God, which human beings can never survey.

We learn the sense of the logical operators by being trained to *use* statements containing them, i.e., to assert such statements under certain conditions. Thus we learn to assert ⌜P and Q⌝ when we can assert P and can assert Q; to assert ⌜P or Q⌝ when we can assert P or can assert Q; to assert ⌜For some n, F (n)⌝ when we can assert ⌜F (o)⌝ or can assert ⌜F (1)⌝ or .... We learn to assert ⌜For every n, F (n)⌝ when we can assert ⌜F (o)⌝ and ⌜F (1)⌝ and ...; and to say that we can assert all of these means that we have a general method for establishing ⌜F (x)⌝ irrespective of the value of x. Here we have abandoned altogether the attempt to explain the meaning of a statement by laying down its truth-conditions. *We no longer explain the sense of a statement by stipulating its truth-value in terms of the truth-values of its constituents, but by stipulating when it may be asserted in terms of the conditions under which its constituents may be asserted.* The justification for this change is that this is how we in fact learn to use these statements: furthermore, the notions of truth and falsity cannot be satisfactorily explained so as to form a basis for an account of meaning once we leave the realm of effectively decidable statements. One result of this shift in our account of meaning is that, unless we are dealing only with effectively decidable statements, certain formulas which appeared in the two-valued logic to be logical laws no longer rank as such, in particular the law of excluded middle: this is rejected, not on the ground that there is a middle truth-value, but because meaning, and hence validity, is no longer to be explained in terms of truth-values.

Intuitionists speak of mathematics in a highly anti-realist (anti-platonist) way: for them it is *we* who construct mathematics; it is not already *there* waiting for us to discover. An extreme form of such constructivism is found in Wittgenstein's *Remarks on the Foundations of Mathematics*. This makes it appear as though the intuitionist rejection of an account of the meaning of mathematical statements in terms of truth and falsity could not be generalized for other regions of discourse, since even if there is no independent mathematical reality answering to our mathematical statements, there is an independent reality answering to statements of other kinds. On the other hand the exposition of intuitionism I have just given was not based on a rejection of the Fregean notion of a mathematical reality waiting to be discovered, but only on considerations about meaning. Now certainly someone who accepts the intuitionist standpoint in mathematics will not be inclined to adopt the platonist picture. Must he then go to the other extreme, and have the picture of our creating mathematics as we go along? To adopt this picture involves thinking with Wittgenstein that we are *free* in mathematics at every point; no step we take has been forced on us by a necessity external to us, but has been freely chosen. This picture is not the only alternative. If we think that mathematical results are in some sense imposed on us from without, we could have instead the picture of a mathematical reality not already in existence but as it were coming into being as we probe. Our investigations bring into existence what was not there before, but what they bring into existence is not of our own making.

Whether this picture is right or wrong for mathematics, it is available for other regions of reality as an alternative to the realist conception of the world. This shows how it is possible to hold that the intuitionist substitution of an account of the *use* of a statement for an account of its truth-conditions as the general form of explanation of meaning should be applied to all realms of discourse without thinking that we create the world; we can abandon realism without falling into subjective idealism. This substitution does not, of course, involve dropping the words 'true' and 'false', since for most ordinary contexts the account of these words embodied in the laws 'It is true that p if and only if p' and 'It is false that p if and only if not p' is quite sufficient: but it means facing the consequences of admitting that this is the *whole* explanation of the sense of these words, and this involves dethroning truth and falsity from their central place in philosophy and in particular in the theory of meaning. Of course the doctrine that meaning is to be explained in terms of use is the cardinal doctrine of the later Wittgenstein; but I do not think the point of this doctrine has so far been generally understood.

IV

SINGULAR TERMS AND PREDICATION

P. F. STRAWSON

THE ideas of *singular term* and of *general term in predicative position* play a central part in Quine's theory of canonical notation. I examine two attempts to explain these ideas, and I argue that they rest upon certain other notions whose role as foundations is not clearly acknowledged in Quine's explanations.

I

In his new book[1] Quine distinguishes once more between singular terms and general terms. He also speaks of different 'positions' which terms may occupy in sentences, notably of referential and of predicative position. 'Referential', or 'purely referential', position is more narrowly understood by Quine than 'position for a singular term'; and if, later on in what follows, I appear to ignore this fact, my reasons are: (1) that I may do so without risk of confusion since I shall not be concerned with, or introduce, any of those referentially opaque contexts which yield positions for singular terms other than purely referential positions; and (2) that 'referential position' is a more convenient expression than 'position for a singular term'.

The relations between these notions of terms and positions are not altogether simple; but fortunately it appears from Quine's exposition that there is one quite fundamental distinction a grasp of which will serve as the basis for everything else. This is the distinction between a *singular term* on the one hand and a *general term in predicative position* on the other. A union of the two is necessary and sufficient for a fundamental kind, though not perhaps the most primitive kind, of sentence of ordinary language; and in canonical notation, where the only singular terms are variables, a union of the two is necessary and sufficient to yield an atomic open sentence such as all true or false

---

From *Journal of Philosophy*, Vol. 58, No. 15 (1961), pp. 393–412. Reprinted by permission of the author and the *Journal of Philosophy*.

[1] *Word and Object* [see Bibliography]. Page references are given in parentheses. Italics are mine, except where otherwise indicated.

sentences are obtained from by quantification and other devices of sentence composition.

The fundamental distinction can, in fact, be yet more narrowly specified. Quine distinguishes between definite and indefinite singular terms. (Examples of definite singular terms are 'Leo', 'that lion', 'the lion', and, sometimes, 'he' and 'it'; examples of indefinite singular terms are 'everything', 'something', 'every lion', 'some lion', and, sometimes, 'a lion'.) This is not merely a distinction of kind, of species within a genus. It is more like a distinction of senses of the phrase 'singular term'. Definite singular terms are singular terms in the primary sense; indefinite singular terms are singular only in a secondary or derivative sense. Part of the evidence for this comes from Quine's own incidental remarks in which, e.g., he contrasts indefinite singular terms, as being '*dummy* singular terms', with '*ordinary* or definite ones' (112–114). But more decisive than these passing remarks is the character of Quine's explanations. The explanation of the fundamental distinction in role between *singular term* and *general term in predicative position* is an explanation which has to be understood as applying only to *definite* singular terms. The *position* which definite singular terms occupy, when they play a certain characteristic role in predication, may also be occupied by other terms which do not play this characteristic role, but are allowed the *title* of singular terms just because they can occupy this position; and these are the dummy or indefinite singular terms.

The basic distinction we have to consider, then, is between *definite singular terms* on the one hand and *general terms in predicative position* on the other. Before we look at Quine's explanation of it, let us note a negative remark he makes about the distinction between singular and general terms at large. He points out that this distinction does not consist in each singular term's having application to just one object while each general term has application to more than one. That the difference does not consist in this is, he says, evident from the fact that some singular terms such as 'Pegasus', may apply to nothing at all, while some general terms such as 'natural satellite of the earth' may each apply to just one thing. There is another reason, which Quine does not mention, for rejecting this account of the difference. 'The captain is angry' is a sentence containing the singular term 'the captain' and the general term 'angry' in predicative position. If we consider at large the two terms 'the captain' and 'angry', it is obvious that *both* of them *have application* to, may be correctly applied to, *many* things; and may be so applied by the use, among others, of this very sentence. If, on the other hand, we think of this sentence as used to make a particular assertion on a particular occasion, it is evident that *both* the singular and the general term, on that particular occasion, are equally *being applied* to *just one* (and the same) thing. Neither way of taking the expressions brings out a difference which we can express in terms of the difference between applying (or being applied) to just one thing and applying (or being applied) to more than one thing.

Quine mentions another way, which he also thinks unsatisfactory, of trying to bring out the difference between definite singular terms and general terms in predicative position. One adopts this way in saying that the singular term *purports* to refer to just one object while the general term does not: even if the general term, like 'natural satellite of the earth' in fact has singularity of reference, this singularity of reference is not something *purported* in the term. Of this way of explaining the difference Quine says: "Such talk of purport is only a picturesque way of alluding to the distinctive grammatical roles that singular and general terms play in sentences. It is by grammatical role that singular and general terms are properly to be distinguished" (96). Elsewhere, discussing the notion of referential position (i.e., the position occupied by a definite singular term when it plays its characteristic, distinctive role in predication), he speaks of the "intuitive" idea behind this notion as the idea that the term occupying this position "is used purely to specify its object for the rest of the sentence to say something about" (177). Quine is right in thinking that these descriptions which he calls "picturesque" or "intuitive" are unsatisfactory. They are unsatisfactory not because they are intuitive or picturesque, but because they are inaccurate or unclear or both. Nevertheless we shall see that they may be inaccurate and unclear attempts to express an idea which is essential to full understanding of Quine's own explanation of the 'distinctive roles' of general and singular terms and yet is an idea to which he himself scarcely succeeds in giving a clear expression.

I turn now to Quine's explanation. It runs: "The basic combination in which general and singular terms find their contrasting roles is that of *predication*[1] . . . Predication joins a general term and a singular term to form a sentence that is true or false according as the general term is true or false of the object, if any, to which the singular term refers" (96). This is supposed to be a description of a contrast of grammatical

---

[1] Quine's italics.

roles; the dichotomy of terms that Quine is concerned with is supposed to be "clarified" by this description of roles (97). Distinctions of grammatical *form* are associated with this contrast of roles: e.g., grammar requires that the predicative role be signalized by the form of the verb; if the general term does not already possess this form, it must, to be fitted for predicative position, be prefixed with the copula 'is' or 'is a (n)' (96–97). But it is the distinction of role thus signalized, and not the form of signalling, that is important for logical theory.

But what is this distinction? The passage I quoted seems to envisage a situation in which there is, on the one hand, a sentence formed by joining two terms and in which there may or may not be, on the other hand, an object to which both terms are correctly applied. The difference in role of the two terms might be held to be shown by the implied differences between the ways in which there might fail to be such an object. Thus the failure might, so to speak, be justly laid at the door of the general term; but only if (1) there indeed was a certain object to which the singular term was correctly applied, and (2) the general term failed to apply to *that* object, i.e., *the* object to which the singular term was correctly applied. It is implied that in this case of failure the sentence (statement) is false. Or again the failure might be justly laid at the door of the singular term; but this would be quite a different kind of failure. It would not be a failure of the singular term to apply to *the object which* . . . —where this 'which' clause could be filled out by mentioning the general term. The failure of application of the singular term would not, like that of its partner, depend on its partner's success. It would be a quite independent failure. And it appears to be here implied, and it is elsewhere stated, that the result of this failure would be not that the sentence was to be assessed as false, but that it was not to be assessed for truth value at all. Whether the sentence is true or false depends on the success or failure of the general term; but the failure of the singular term appears to deprive the general term of the chance of either success or failure.

If this is a correct reading of Quine's sentence, then it is clear that the description he gives of the crucial distinction is designed to fit at most (on the side of singular terms) only *definite* singular terms; for it contains no attempt to mention any contrast there may be *in role or function* between indefinite singular terms and general terms in predicative position. Quine's complementary account of such a sentence as '*A comet* was *observed by astronomers tonight*', containing one indefinite singular term and one composite general term in predicative position, would be that it is true if there is an object, any object, to which both terms apply; otherwise false. In respect of *role* the two terms are not distinguished at all. If we ask why one of the two terms is nevertheless to be called a singular term and the other not, we may indeed appeal to grammar; but it will now be an appeal to what Quine contrasts with grammatical *role*, viz., to grammatical *form*. The term 'a comet' is formally like a (definite) singular term in that it is a substantive occupying the position of grammatical subject to the predicative copula (a special case of the verb of predication in general). It is formally unlike a general term in predicative position in that it has no predicative copula prefixed to it and does not itself possess the form of a verb. In no other way mentioned by Quine does it differ from the general term. As for 'everything' and 'something', the description leaves us to presume that they are entitled to classification as singular terms in so far as they too may occupy this position, may share these formal characteristics.

If my reading of Quine's sentence is correct, there is a much more important point to be made. It is that the distinction drawn remains inadequately explained. The explanation raises, rather than answers, questions. "Predication joins a general term and a singular term to form a sentence ... "—a sentence in which the two kinds of term exhibit the obscure differences I have set out. But what is it that *accounts* for these differences? Unless we can answer this question, we shall certainly not fully understand the distinction; indeed we shall scarcely know what predication is. We cannot give up the question and be content with talk of verbs and substantives, of grammatical subjects and predicates. Quine is no more one of Ramsey's schoolchildren doing English grammar than Ramsey himself was. But neither can we be satisfied with the distinction as I have interpreted it. Singular terms are what yield truth-value gaps when they fail in their role. General terms are what yield truth or falsity, when singular terms succeed in their role, by themselves applying, or failing to apply, to what the singular terms apply to. This is more or less what we have. It scarcely seems enough. We want to ask 'Why?'

It might be objected at this point that my interpretation of Quine's sentence was perverse, that the cumbrousness and obscurity of the reading were quite unnecessary. In Quine's sentence there occur the two contrasting expressions, 'is true of', associated with the general term, and 'refers to', associated with the singular term; and this contrast I have deliberately ignored, contenting myself with the single expression 'applies to'. May not this difference of expression, which

I ignored, be intended to reflect a difference in the ways in which singular and general terms respectively apply or are applied to objects? And may not the explanation we are still seeking be found in this difference of mode of application?

This seems a reasonable suggestion. But there are several reasons why we cannot be content simply to *repeat* these expressions, to say 'In the successful predication, the singular term *refers* to its object, while the general term is *true of* it'. For one thing, Quine himself does not adhere consistently to this usage. On page 95 he writes ' "Pegasus" counts as a singular term though *true of* nothing'; and on pages 108–109 he repeatedly uses the idioms of *being true of* and *referring* (*having reference*) *to* interchangeably in connexion with general terms. This point is not very important. Even if Quine had been perfectly consistent in his usage, it would still be the case that the difference in force between the expressions 'is true of' and 'refers to' calls as loudly for explanation as the expressions 'general term' and 'singular term' themselves. Neither pair, unaided, serves to explain the other. This is why I ignored the difference of expression and used instead the undifferentiated idiom of *application*. The deliberate nondifferentiation of expression diminishes the risk of our seeming to understand a distinction when we do not.

This is the point at which we have to return to ideas of the kind that Quine dismissed as vague and picturesque. Let us consider those predications in which singular and general term alike may fairly be said to be applied to a single concrete and spatio-temporally continuous object (e.g., 'Mama is kind', 'That picture is valuable', 'The doctor is coming to dinner'). What is the characteristic difference in the mode in which they are applied? Let us recall that, in such a predication, neither of the terms employed need be such that it *applies* to only one object, though both are currently *being applied to* just one object, and, if all goes well, both do in fact *apply* to that object. Now what is the characteristic difference between the relations of the two terms to the object? The characteristic difference, I suggest, is that the singular term is used for the purpose of *identifying* the object, of bringing it about that the hearer (or, generally, the audience) knows *which* or *what* object is in question; while the general term is not. It is enough if the general term in fact applies to the object; it does not also have to identify it.

But what exactly is this task of identifying an object for a hearer? Well, let us consider that in any communication situation a hearer (an audience) is antecedently equipped with a certain amount of knowledge, with certain presumptions, with a certain range of possible current perception. There are within the scope of his knowledge or present perception objects which he is able *in one way or another* to distinguish for himself. The identificatory task of *one* of the terms, in predications of the kind we are now concerned with, is to bring it about that the hearer knows *which* object it is, of all the objects within the hearer's scope of knowledge or presumption, that the *other* term is being applied to. This identificatory task is characteristically the task of the definite singular term. That term achieves its identificatory purpose by drawing upon what in the widest sense might be called the conditions of its utterance, *including* what the hearer is presumed to know or to presume already or to be in a position there and then to perceive for himself. This is not something incidental to the use of singular terms in predications of the kind we are now concerned with. It is quite central to this use. The possibility of identification in the relevant sense exists only for an audience antecedently equipped with knowledge or presumptions, or placed in a position of possible perception, which can be drawn on in this way.[1]

Perhaps the phrase about purporting singularity of application that Quine found unsatisfactory should be construed as a shot at describing the identificatory function of singular terms. If so, Quine was right to think it unsatisfactory. Not only is the phrase far from clear. But at least one fairly natural sense that it might bear is foreign to the purpose. Thus an expression might be said to 'purport singularity of application' if it contained phrases making express uniqueness claims, phrases such as 'the only', 'unique in', 'alone', 'just one'. But terms used for the identificatory purpose will rarely contain such phrases. Such phrases will more naturally occur where the purpose on hand is a different one: e.g., to inform a hearer, with regard to some

---

[1] A full account of the matter would call for much more detail and many qualifications. I cannot claim to be doing more than drawing attention to a *characteristic* difference of function between definite singular terms and general terms in predicative position, in cases where both terms alike may fairly be said to be applied to a single concrete object. Thus it would not be true to say that the use of a definite singular term for a particular is *always* designed to draw upon resources of identifying knowledge or presumption antecedently in possession of the audience. For *sometimes* the operations of supplying such resources and of drawing on them may be conflated in the use of a singular term. Nor would it be true to say the general term is *never* used, whereas the singular term is *always* used, for the purpose of indicating to the audience which object it is that the other term is being applied to. For it is easy to think of cases in which, as one would be inclined to say, the roles are reversed. But counter-examples to a universal thesis about differences of function are not necessarily counter-examples to a thesis about characteristic difference of function. We must *weigh* our examples, and not treat them *simply* as counters.

independently identified object, that it is unique in a certain respect, or to inform him that *there is* something unique in a certain respect. But then the expressions containing such phrases do not have the characteristic role of definite singular terms. They can, as Quine would say, readily be parsed as general terms in predicative position.

Slightly better, but still unsatisfactory, is Quine's alternative description of 'the intuitive idea behind *purely referential position*', viz., "that the term is used purely to specify its object for the rest of the sentence to say something about". Still unsatisfactory, since 'specify' by itself remains vague. To remove the vagueness we need the concept of 'identifying for an audience' which I have just introduced. Fully to elucidate *this* idea a great deal more should be said about the conditions and means of such identification. But we have enough for our immediate purposes: enough to see that a real difference of function is reflected by the difference between the expressions 'refers to' and 'is true of', and that these expressions, used as Quine uses them, are not inappropriate; and enough to understand why Quine should impute the differences that he seems by implication to impute to the nature and consequences of application failure on the part of singular and general terms, respectively.

It is easy enough to see why the distinction of function should lead philosophers to this further distinction. It happens something like this. Let us suppose that the identificatory function has been successfully performed. The successful performance of this function does not, of course, settle the question of the truth or falsity of the predication as a whole. What settles that question would seem to be whether or not the general term applies to the object, whether, as Quine would say, it is true or false *of* the object. But now suppose a radical failure of identificatory function. By a radical failure I mean, not simply the use of an incorrect instead of a correct designation; nor simply the use of a designation which, correct or incorrect, fails to invoke appropriate knowledge in the possession of the hearer and hence leaves him in the dark as to which object is being referred to, or causes him to mistake the identity of that object. I mean the case (rare enough) when there is no appropriate *knowledge*, in anyone's possession, to be invoked; where all such supposed knowledge is not knowledge, but mistake; where there just is no such object as the singular term is supposed to identify. This situation is indeed different from the situation in which the general term simply does not in fact apply to the successfully identified object. We think of the predication as a whole as true in the case where the general term does apply to the object that the singular term is supposed to identify. We think of the predication as a whole as false in the case where the general term does *not* apply to that object, the case where the general term can be truthfully *denied* of that object. But the case where there is no such object is neither a case where the general term can be truly affirmed of it nor a case where the general term can be truly denied of it. Hence there is a strong inclination to say that the predication as a whole is neither true nor false in this case (even that there is no predication at all in this case). Some philosophers have resisted this inclination, and have argued in favour of classifying this case together with the case in which the general term fails to apply to the successfully identified object, under the common appellation, 'false'. There has been debate over this, and it has sometimes seemed that the debate over the use of the word 'false' was the really substantial question, on the answer to which hung all the other debated issues in this area. But this is not so; for many reasons. The claim that the radical failure of a definite singular term results in a truth-value gap is in some cases more intuitively satisfactory, in others less intuitively satisfactory, than the claim that it results in falsity. This is not a mere oddity or 'quirk' of intuition (or usage). It is something that can be explained; though not here and now.[1]

But, however *that* is explained, it remains important that the identificatory function of singular terms should be acknowledged, seen for what it is, and clearly distinguished from the operation of asserting that there is just one thing answering to certain specifications. This distinction is implicitly denied by Russell, at least as far as some classes of singular terms are concerned. It is, on the other hand, implicitly acknowledged by Quine; and to that extent I am with Quine. My present reproach against him is contained in the word 'implicitly'. For when we read that key sentence of his, designed to elucidate the functional distinction between singular and general terms, we are constrained to read it as an obscure statement of a debated consequence of that distinction rather than as a description of the distinction itself; while those more hopeful phrases that might seem to point, however waveringly, in the right direction, are dismissed as vague, intuitive, or picturesque instead of being used as stepping-stones towards the definite, the explicit, and the literal. What makes this the more surprising is that, in the course of some remarks devoted to the discussion of different types of singular terms, Quine shows himself well enough aware of the identifying function of singular terms in

[1] [See the author's 'Identifying Reference and Truth-Values', *Theoria* (1964). Ed.]

general. I content myself with two quotations: 'In "I saw the lion" the singular term "the lion" is presumed to refer to some one lion, *distinguished from its fellows* for speaker and hearer by previous sentences or attendant circumstances' (112). 'In ordinary discourse the idiom of . . . singular description is normally used only where *the intended object* is believed to be *singled out uniquely* by the matter appended to the singular "the" together perhaps with supplementary information . . .' (183). These idioms of 'singling out' or 'distinguishing' the 'intended' object are all in the right spirit. And on page 103 there even occurs, just once, the key word 'identification'.

There are, of course, as Quine's discussion shows, many different types of situation in which the identificatory function is performed and many different types of resource upon which a speaker may draw or rely in performing it. He may draw upon what the speaker can be presumed to be in a position then and there to see or otherwise perceive for himself. He may rely upon information imparted by earlier sentences in the same conversation. He may rely upon information in the hearer's possession which is not derived from either of these sources, or upon past experience and recognitional capacities of the hearer's which the latter could scarcely articulate into a description. He may draw or rely upon any combination of these. But he *must* draw upon something in this area if the identificatory function is to be performed at all. That function is successfully performed if and only if the singular term used establishes for the hearer an identity, and the right identity, between the thought of *what-is-being-spoken-of-by-the-speaker* and the thought of some object *already within the reach of the hearer's own knowledge, experience, or perception*, some object, that is, which the hearer could, in one way or another, pick out or identify for himself, from his own resources. To succeed in its task, the singular term, together with the circumstances of its utterance, must draw on the appropriate stretch of those resources.

Is there anything in what I have so far said that Quine would wish or need to dispute? I think the answer is a qualified negative. Had I asked this question about Russell, it seems that the answer should be an unqualified affirmative. For Russell appears to claim for the Theory of Descriptions that it gives an exact account of the working of one class of definite singular terms, viz., singular descriptions. And I am bound to deny this. For in the analysis of singular descriptions given in the Theory of Descriptions the identificatory function of singular terms is suppressed altogether. Its place is taken by an explicit assertion to the effect that there exists just one thing with a certain property. But to say this is to do something quite different from identifying that thing for a hearer in the sense I have been concerned with. One who says that there exists just one thing with a certain property typically intends to inform his hearer of this fact. Thereby he does indeed supply the hearer with resources of knowledge which constitute, so to speak, a minimal basis for a subsequent identifying reference to draw on. But the act of supplying new resources is not the same act as the act of drawing on independently established resources.

The non-identity of these acts, on the other hand, constitutes no *prima facie* objection to Quine's proposal for the elimination of definite singular terms from 'canonical notation'. For Quine does not claim that the sentences which replace those containing definite singular terms have the same meaning as the latter (182). Nor, presumably, would he claim that they would normally serve exactly the same purpose; for this, if I am right, would be to claim too much. He would claim that in some weaker sense the sentences containing singular terms could be replaced by the sentences in canonical notation. What this weaker kind of substitutability is we need not here inquire too closely, if we suppose merely that it is not such as to conflict with the account I have sketched of the characteristic identificatory function of definite singular terms. There remains a point of more immediate significance concerning our understanding of the apparatus of theoretical notions within the framework of which the idea of canonical notation is introduced. The relevant part of Quine's programme of paraphrase can most simply be summed up as follows. All *terms* other than the variables of quantification will be found, in canonical notation, to be general terms in predicative position. The *position* of singular terms is reserved for the quantifiers and the variables of quantification; and since quantifiers themselves do not count as *terms*, the only singular terms left are the variables of quantification. But, merely formal distinctions of grammar apart, how was the distinction between *singular terms* and *general terms in predicative position* explained? It was explained in terms of the contrasting roles in predication of the *definite* singular term and the general term in predicative position. This contrast of roles is our fundamental clue to all the theoretical notions employed. So our theoretical grasp of the nature of canonical notation rests upon our theoretical grasp of the identificatory function of singular terms. And this is why Quine should have elucidated more fully than he did those notions which he was content to dismiss as vague and picturesque.

II

It may be retorted at this point that it is not necessary for Quine to present his distinction of terms and positions as resting on the contrasting roles in predication of the definite singular term and the general term in predicative position. There is, it may be said, a way of presenting the distinction which is independent of any appeal to the function of the definite singular term; and it is a way which Quine sometimes makes use of. The position of a singular term in general can be directly explained as position accessible to quantifiers and variables of quantification or to those expressions of ordinary language to which quantifiers and variables correspond. Predicative position, on the other hand, is inaccessible to quantifiers. It is occupied by general terms which complement quantifiers (or other occupants of singular-term position) to yield sentences. All we need now assume is that we can understand the role of quantifiers or of those idioms of ordinary language which the quantifiers 'encapsulate'. If we can assume this much understanding, we have materials for explaining the concepts of singular term and of predicative position; and the general programme can proceed without the intelligibility of its whole apparatus of theoretical notions appearing to rest on our grasp of the functioning of definite singular terms.

This way out proves delusive; and in observing just how it proves delusive, we shall see how the account I gave in Part I of this paper itself needs to be deepened and strengthened. Predicative position is supposed to be inaccessible to quantifiers. But is it? Betty is a better date than Sally. Betty is willing and pretty and Sally too is willing and pretty. But Betty is also witty and Sally is not witty. Surely, it seems, 'willing', 'pretty', and 'witty' are here in predicative position. But is their position inaccessible to quantifiers? As a date, Betty is everything that Sally is (i.e., willing and pretty) and something that Sally isn't (i.e., witty). Or, if you like, there is nothing that Sally is that Betty isn't and something that Sally isn't that Betty is.

What are we to do? Are we to stick by the test without qualification and say that the example shows that 'witty' and 'pretty' are singular terms, and 'Sally' and 'Betty' are in predicative position? This will attract no one, and anyway would obliterate the distinction altogether, since the test could be differently, and more obviously, applied to yield the conclusion that 'Sally' and 'Betty' were singular terms, and 'witty' and 'pretty' were in predicative position.

Are we to try to save the situation by saying that the test for being a singular term includes not only occupancy of a position accessible to quantifiers but also the possession of the grammatical form of the substantive? But this *by itself* would be the wrong kind of appeal to grammar, the kind that Quine would rightly repudiate. Can we buttress this additional requirement with a supposed rationale for it, saying that what it really amounts to is the requirement that the term displaced by the quantifier, if a definite term, should designate an *object*, and that 'Betty' satisfies this requirement while 'pretty' does not? But other objections apart, how shall we then deal with the 'offenders', as Quine calls them (240), who stoutly affirm that 'witty' and 'pretty' in 'Sally is pretty' and 'Betty is witty' *do* designate objects, namely attributes? Quine's general method of dealing with such offenders is not available here. For to one who says (roughly) that the use of any term commits its user to a corresponding object Quine is wont to reply (roughly) that this is so only where the term occupies a position that it can yield to a quantifier. But the trouble with the terms in question here is that they do occupy positions that they can yield to quantifiers. So we are back where we started.

Let us think again about our example, and in a spirit as sympathetic to Quine as possible. Suppose we redescribe the situation as follows. Prettiness is a quality desirable in a date and Betty has prettiness and Sally has prettiness. Similarly with willingness. Wit is a quality desirable in a date and Betty has wit and Sally has not. Everything which Sally has and which is a quality desirable in a date is something which Betty has; but there is something which is a quality desirable in a date and which Betty has, which Sally does not have. I think that Quine would say that this form of description of the situation is a better, a more logically candid, form than the first. But how does it differ from the first? Well, it differs in that the terms that yield their positions to quantifiers have the grammatical form of substantives and not of adjectives. But we are agreed not to regard this as a vital difference. A more significant difference is this. There is something explicit in the second account of the situation that was only implicit in the first; and it is made explicit by the use of the expression 'quality desirable in a date'.[1] Let us try to follow this clue. It gives us the following result. 'Prettiness' occupies singular-term, or referential, position because it is joined with such an expression as 'desirable in a date', which, relative to it, occupies predicative position. Generally, whenever, explicitly or implicitly, two terms are joined of which the

---

[1] Cf. Quine, p. 119: 'The move that ushers in abstract singular terms has to be one that simultaneously ushers in abstract general ones.'

first stands to the second in that characteristic relation in which 'prettiness' (or 'pretty') stands to 'desirable in a date', then, relatively to each other, the first is a candidate for referential and the second for predicative position. Thus, even in our first description of the situation, 'pretty' had implicitly referential position. It did not have implicitly referential position considered simply in relation to 'Sally' (or 'Betty'). Rather it was a candidate for predicative position relative to 'Sally'. For it does not stand to 'Sally' as it stands to 'desirable in a date' but rather as 'desirable in a date' stands to it. But it still had implicitly referential position; for it was *implied* that being pretty was desirable in a date. And it was because it had implicitly *referential* position that it could comfortably yield its position to quantification.

But now let us ponder this. A new criterion seems to have emerged for the relative concept of referential and predicative positions. I shall call it the type-criterion. (Elsewhere I have called it—or, rather, its basis—the category-criterion.)[1] 'Pretty' has predicative significance relative to 'Betty', referential significance relative to 'desirable in a date'. We have a series consisting of (1) 'Betty', (2) 'pretty' or 'prettiness', (3) 'desirable in a date', such that any earlier term in the series is a candidate for referential position relative to the immediately succeeding term, and any later term is a candidate for predicative position relative to the immediately preceding term.[2] But what is the general nature of such a series, what is it about its terms and their relations that confers upon them these further relations, these claims to relative referential and predicative position? Well, it will scarcely be denied that 'Betty' is typically used to designate a spatio-temporally continuous particular. And it will scarcely be denied that the meaning of 'pretty' is such that it may be said to *group* such particulars in accordance with a certain kind of principle. The term may be said to group all those particulars whose designations may be coupled with it to yield true statements. Now in a certain sense 'Betty' may be said to group particulars too: a particular arm, leg, face, even a particular action, might all be truthfully ascribed to Betty. But obviously the principle on which 'Betty' groups particulars like arms and legs is quite a different sort of principle from the principle on which 'pretty'

---

[1] See *Individuals*, ch. 5 *et seq.*

[2] The variation in form from 'pretty' to 'prettiness' supplies the substantive which is grammatically typical for referential position; the insertion of 'has' before 'prettiness' yields a phrase which as a whole is grammatically suitable for predicative position, while containing a part, 'prettiness', grammatically suitable for referential position.

groups particulars like Betty and Sally. Now consider such a term as (3) 'desirable in a date'. This term has a grouping function too. It does not directly group particulars; it groups *ways*, such as term (2)'s way, *of grouping particulars*. But there are analogies and connexions between term (3)'s way of grouping ways of grouping particulars and term (2)'s way of grouping particulars. The principle that term (3) supplies, of grouping ways of grouping, is like the principle that term (2) supplies, of grouping particulars, in a way in which both are quite unlike the principle of grouping particulars that term (1) supplies. These likenesses and unlikenesses are registered in the terminology of philosophy: in the series that starts with *particular*, and goes on with *property or kind of particulars*, *property or kind of property or kind of particular*, etc.; in the philosophical usage which permits us to say that Betty is a case or instance of prettiness, and prettiness a case or instance of a quality desirable in a date, but forbids us to say that Betty's left arm or anything else is a case or instance of Betty.[1]

The result, then, of our reflections on our example is this. Two terms coupled in a true sentence stand in referential and predicative position, respectively, if what the first term designates or signifies is a case or instance of what the second term signifies. Items thus related (or the terms that designate or signify them) may be said respectively to be of lower and of higher type; and this is why I called the new criterion one of type.[2] Part of the explanation of the kind of group-

[1] Not all particulars are spatio-temporally *continuous* as Betty is. But the contrast between principles of grouping is not in general dependent on such continuity, though it is seen most easily in cases characterized by continuity. The expression 'The Plough' (used as the name of a constellation) designates a spatio-temporal particular, though not a continuous one; whereas even if it should come to pass that all the gold in the universe formed one continuous mass, this would not turn 'gold' into the designation of a spatio-temporal particular. What makes it correct to count a star as a bit of the Plough or an arm as a bit of Betty has at least to do with their spatio-temporal relation to other bits of the Plough or of Betty in a way in which what makes it correct to count something as an instance of gold has nothing to do with its spatio-temporal relations to other instances of gold. The distinction between *being a particular part of* (or *element in*, etc.) and *being a particular instance of* remains bright enough here, even though spatial continuity is gone. Of course this is only the beginning of a long and complex story which perhaps has no very clear and definite end; for as we bring more sophisticated characters into our story, the clarity and the simplicity of the contrast between principles of grouping tend to diminish. But we are investigating foundations; and it is enough if the beginnings are clear and distinct.

[2] But, of course, by adopting this terminology I by no means intend to suggest that the only differences that can properly be described as differences of type or category are the very broad differences I am concerned with. One may have occasion, for example, to distinguish many different types or categories *within* the very broad category of particulars.

ing which terms of higher type than the lowest can do was that it is a kind of grouping which designations of spatio-temporal particulars *cannot* do. So implicit in this criterion of relative position is the consequence that a term designating a particular can never occupy predicative position. A term signifying a kind or property, however, may occupy referential or predicative position, depending upon whether it is, or is not, coupled with a term of still higher type.

Now it might be maintained that we do not need this criterion in addition to the identificatory criterion suggested in Part I of this paper. It was there suggested that the primary occupant of referential position was the term which served to identify the object both terms applied to, the object the sentence was about. Does not this criterion work as well for 'Prettiness is a quality desirable in a date' as it does for 'Betty is pretty'? Just as 'Betty' identifies, and 'pretty' does not, the object the second sentence is about, so 'prettiness' identifies, and 'quality desirable in a date' does not, the attribute the first sentence is about. But before we acquiesce too readily in this suggestion, let us consider more carefully the way in which, both here and originally, we *applied* the identificatory criterion. When we do so, we see that the *type-criterion was already implicit in our application of the identificatory criterion*. We said that 'Betty' identifies, and 'pretty' does not, the object the sentence is about; what the sentence tells us about Betty is that she is *pretty*. But in saying this we have already shown a tacit preference for the particular, the item of lower (lowest) type, as the object the sentence is about. There is nothing in the word 'about' or in the concept of identification in general to compel this *exclusive* choice. We could equally well say (and in some contexts it would be correct to say) that the sentence was about prettiness; and that what it says about prettiness is that *Betty* is pretty. The term 'pretty' identifies the attribute the sentence is about; the words 'Betty is' inform us where the attribute is to be found. But though there was nothing in the word 'about' or in the concept of identification in general that compelled this exclusive preference, nevertheless there was something that compelled it: this was the conjunction of the two facts: first, that we were seeking to elucidate the distinction between referential and predicative position, and, second, that the type-criterion is essential to this distinction. This does not mean that we should abandon the identificatory criterion. It only means that we should acknowledge that the exclusive way in which it is applied reflects our acceptance of the type-criterion.

We fuse the two, to obtain the following account of the distinction between referential and predicative position, an account which, if I am right, underlies all that Quine says about this distinction. Referential position is the position primarily and fundamentally occupied by a term definitely identifying a spatio-temporal particular in a sentence coupling that term to another signifying a property-like or kind-like principle of grouping particulars. The particular-identifying term is the primary case of a definite singular term. The other term occupies predicative position. Second, referential position may be occupied by a term signifying a property-like or kind-like principle of grouping particulars provided that this term is itself coupled to another term which signifies a higher principle of grouping such principles of gouping. The first of these terms is then a secondary case of a definite singular term. The other term again occupies predicative position. Finally, the position occupied by a definite singular term of any kind may be coherently yielded to a kind of term which does not characteristically have the identifying function of a definite singular term, and which is called an indefinite singular term.

The above sentences of mine by no means constitute a complete account of the distinction between referential and predicative position, between singular term and general term in predicative position. But they provide, perhaps, the necessary basis on which, by further extension, analogy, and qualification, any complete account must be built.

But now what has happened to quantification? We set out with the suggestion that accessibility to quantifiers might provide a test for referential position independent of the explanations of Part I. We end by returning to the explanations of Part I, with the addition of an explicit awareness of the type-criterion they implicitly involved. Quantification seems to have disappeared from view altogether. Yet quantifiers were supposed to hold the key to referential position. How are we to explain this?

We can understand the situation better if we remember that quantification is also supposed by Quine to hold the key to something else, viz., the ontological commitments of our talk. Quantifiers hold the key to ontic commitment because the objects are "what count as cases when, quantifying, we say that everything or something is thus-and-so" (240). They hold the key to referential position because they encapsulate certain "specially selected, unequivocally referential idioms of ordinary language", viz., 'there is an object x such that' and 'every object x is such that' (242). Here the notions of *object, reference,* and *quantification* seem to stand in firm connexion without any dependence on the ideas of type and of identification that I have invoked. But let us look a little more closely: at the tell-tale word 'cases' in the first quotation and at the way in which 'something' and 'thus-and-so' are balanced about the 'is'; at the word 'object' itself in the second quotation. Does the word 'object' itself already contain, concealed, the type-criterion, the preference for particulars? After all, we readily say that spatio-temporally continuous particulars are *objects* and less readily say this of attributes and the rest. Suppose we leave it out, to guard against prejudice. Then why should we prefer 'There is something *that is thus-and-so*' to 'There is something *that such-and-such is*' as the general form of what we say when we use an existential quantifier? The reason is clear; but it leads us straight back to the type-criterion. In a two-term sentence in which one term identifies an item of lower type to which the other term non-identifyingly applies, it is the identifying term for this item that is the grammatical subject of the predicative 'is' and characteristically precedes it. What characteristically follows the 'is' (as grammatical complement) is the term that applies to, but does not identify, the item of lower type; it is the term that signifies (identifies) an item of higher type, that which the item of lower type is being said to be *a case of*.[1] So it is the type-relation, the type-order, that dictates Quine's choice of phrasing, and thereby seems to vindicate the alleged link between quantification and referential position.

This is not to say that the quantification test is a bad test for referential position. On the contrary, it is, on the whole, a good test.[2] But the explanation of its being a good test leads us once more back to the type-criterion. It is a good test because there is never any point in introducing a quantifier into a place that could be occupied by a term signifying an item of a higher type *unless* this is done in coupling with a term signifying an item of a still higher type.[3] Hence quantifiers always occupy relatively lower-type

---

[1] The point can indeed be put, though less clearly, without reference to identification. Something a thing *is* is of a higher type than anything which *is* it; a thing which *is* something is of a lower type than anything it *is*. The italicized 'is' here corresponds to 'is a case of', though it differs from the latter phrase, of course, in permitting a grammatically adjectival termination.

[2] The words 'on the whole' signify the need for certain reservations, or at least for further reflection, about some adverbial expressions like 'here', 'there', 'now', 'then'. Quine says these can be 'parsed' as general terms. But no amount of parsing would seem to defend their position from occupation by 'somewhere', 'somewhen', etc.

[3] The point is explained in *Individuals*. See especially p. 327.

positions. We saw this, in a not very clear way, in the example about the qualities desirable in a date. In 'There is something that Betty is and Sally is not' we appeared to be quantifying in a higher-type region without any coupling to a term of still higher type. But we had to acknowledge that this was mere appearance, that we were operating implicitly with the still higher-type notion of 'quality desirable in a date'. If we were not implicitly operating with a higher-type notion, the sentence would not be worth affirming. The point becomes clearer if we consider a simpler case. Suppose the term 'Socrates' identifies the philosopher. Then 'There is something that Socrates is' is bound to be true, and 'Socrates is everything' (or 'There is nothing Socrates isn't') is bound to be false. There is no point in either sentence if 'Socrates' functions as a singular term identifying the philosopher; just as there is no point in *any* sentence whatever which declares, with regard to any identified item of any type whatever, that it has some property or that it has every property. In general it will never be to the purpose to quantify over items of a higher type unless some still higher-type principle of collection is being implicitly used.

Thus, in practice, the quantification test for referential position is quite a good test. But it is so only because the notions of referential and predicative position (or, if you like, of singular-logical-subject position and logical-predicate position) have to be understood in the way I have outlined. And if I am right in saying that they have to be understood in this way, then I think it must also be admitted that the whole apparatus of distinctions in terms of which the theory of canonical notation is explained rests upon notions whose role is hardly sufficiently acknowledged. The two essential notions are: first, that of an order of types, based upon the quite fundamental distinction between spatio-temporal particulars on the one hand and property-like or kind-like principles of grouping such particulars on the other; and, second, that of the identificatory function characteristically performed by definite singular terms referring to particulars.

The purpose of this paper was to indicate the fundamental place of these two notions in Quine's own thinking about referential and predicative position. That they have this place there is not, as far as I can see, something he would necessarily wish to dispute. But there is, I think, a further and connected consequence, concerning Quine's views on ontology, which is also worth mentioning; and perhaps he would not wish to dispute this either.

The objects to the existence of which our discourse commits us are, according to Quine, the objects, of whatever sort, which "the singular terms, in their several ways, name, refer to, take as values. They are what count as cases when, quantifying, we say that everything, or something, is thus-and-so" (240). Now we have sufficiently seen what the primary objects answering to this description are. They are spatio-temporal particulars And we have seen that this is not something which just happens to be the case. It is a guaranteed consequence of the nature of the fundamental distinction between singular term in referential, and general term in predicative, position. Hence such particulars do not merely happen, for extraneous reasons, to count as objects in Quine's sense. They are the very pattern of objects in this sense. They are not, indeed, the only things that answer to Quine's description. But to say of things of other types that they also answer to this description is simply to say that we have occasion to bring such things under higher principles of grouping, principles which serve to group them in ways analogous to the ways in which expressions signifying properties (or kinds) of particulars serve to group particulars. In so far, then, as things other than spatio-temporal particulars qualify as objects, they do so simply because our thought, our talk, confers upon them the limited and purely logical analogy with spatio-temporal particulars which I have just described. And now, surely, we are in a position to understand the nominalist prejudice, and to discount it—without flattering the fantasies of Platonism. If by accepting as entities, on this logical test, things other than spatio-temporal particulars, we were claiming for them any other, any further, likeness to such particulars than the logical analogy itself contains, we should indeed be running into danger of committing the characteristic category-confusions of Platonist mythology. One who believes that such acceptance inevitably carries such a claim must seem to himself to have every rational motive for the strenuous efforts of paraphrase demanded by a limited and, as nearly as possible, nominalist ontology. But this belief is itself a symptom of confusion. Of course, even when the belief is seen to be illusion, motives of a reasonable kind, elucidatory, aesthetic, for these efforts of paraphrase may still remain. But the motive of metaphysical respectability is gone.

V

PROPER NAMES

JOHN R. SEARLE

Do proper names have senses? Frege[1] argues that they must have senses, for, he asks, how else can identity statements be other than trivially analytic? How, he asks, can a statement of the form a = b, if true, differ in cognitive value from a = a? His answer is that though 'a' and 'b' have the same referent they have or may have different *senses*, in which case the statement is true, though not analytically so. But this solution seems more appropriate where 'a' and 'b' are both non-synonymous definite descriptions, or where one is a definite description and one is a proper name, than where both are proper names. Consider, for example, statements made with the following sentences:

(a) 'Tully = Tully' is analytic.

But is

(b) 'Tully = Cicero' synthetic?

If so, then each name must have a different sense, which seems at first sight most implausible, for we do not ordinarily think of proper names as having a sense at all in the way that predicates do; we do not, e.g. give definitions of proper names. But of course (b) gives us information not conveyed by (a). But is this information about words? The statement is not about words.

For the moment let us consider the view that (b) is, like (a), analytic. A statement is analytic if and only if it is true in virtue of linguistic rules alone, without any recourse to empirical investigation. The linguistic rules for using the name 'Cicero' and the linguistic rules for using the name 'Tully' are such that both names refer to, without describing, the same identical object; thus it seems the truth of the identity can be established solely by recourse to these rules and the statement is analytic. The sense in which the statement is informative is the sense in which any analytic statement is informative; it illustrates or exemplifies certain contingent facts about words, though it does

From *Mind*, Vol. 67 (1958), pp. 166–73. Reprinted by permission of the author and the Editor of *Mind*.

[1] Gottlob Frege, *Philosophical Writings*, translated by Geach and Black, pp. 56 ff.

not of course describe these facts. On this account the difference between (a) and (b) above is not as great as might at first seem. Both are analytically true, and both illustrate contingent facts about our use of symbols. Some philosophers claim that (a) is fundamentally different from (b) in that a statement using this form will be true for any arbitrary substitution of symbols replacing 'Tully'.[1] This, I wish to argue, is not so. The fact that the same mark refers to the same object on two different occasions of its use is a convenient but contingent usage, and indeed we can easily imagine situations where this would not be the case. Suppose, e.g., we have a language in which the rules for using symbols are correlated not simply with a type-word, but with the order of its token appearances in the discourse. Some codes are like this. Suppose the first time an object is referred to in our discourse it is referred to by 'x', the second time by 'y', etc. For anyone who knows this code 'x = y' is trivially analytic, but 'x = x' is senseless. This example is designed to illustrate the similarity of (a) and (b) above; both are analytic and both give us information, though each gives us different information, about the use of words. The truth of the statements that Tully = Tully and Tully = Cicero both follow from linguistic rules. But the fact that the words 'Tully = Tully' are used to express this identity is just as contingent as, though more universally conventional in our language than, the fact that the words 'Tully = Cicero' are used to express the identity of the same object.

This analysis enables us to see how both (a) and (b) could be used to make analytic statements and how in such circumstances we could acquire different information from them, without forcing us to follow either of Frege's proposed solutions, i.e. that the two propositions are in some sense about words (*Begriffsschrift*) or his revised solution, that the terms have the same reference but different senses (*Sinn und Bedeutung*). But though this analysis enables us to see how a sentence like (b) *could* be used to make an analytic statement it does not follow that it could not also be used to make a synthetic statement. And indeed some identity statements using two proper names are clearly synthetic; people who argue that Shakespeare was Bacon are not advancing a thesis about language. In what follows I hope to examine the connexion between proper names and their referents in such a manner as to show how both kinds of identity statement are possible and in so doing to show in what sense a proper name has a sense.

[1] W. V. Quine, *From a Logical Point of View*, esp. chap. 2.

I have so far considered the view that the rules governing the use of a proper name are such that it is used to refer to and not to describe a particular object, that it has reference but not sense. But now let us ask how it comes about that we are able to refer to a particular object by using its name. How, for example, do we learn and teach the use of proper names? This seems quite simple—we identify the object, and, assuming that our student understands the general conventions governing proper names, we explain that this word is the name of that object. But unless our student already knows another proper name of the object, we can only *identify* the object (the necessary preliminary to teaching the name) by ostension or description; and, in both cases, we identify the object in virtue of certain of its characteristics. So now it seems as if the rules for a proper name must somehow be logically tied to particular characteristics of the object in such a way that the name has a sense as well as a reference; indeed, it seems it could not have a reference unless it did have a sense, for how, unless the name has a sense, is it to be correlated with the object?

Suppose someone answers this argument as follows: 'The characteristics located in teaching the name are not the rules for using the proper name: they are simply pedagogic devices employed in teaching the name to someone who does not know how to use it. Once our student has identified the object to which the name applies he can forget or ignore these various descriptions by means of which he identified the object, for they are not part of the sense of the name; the name does not have a *sense*. Suppose, for example, that we teach the name "Aristotle" by explaining that it refers to a Greek philosopher born in Stagira, and suppose that our student continues to use the name correctly, that he gathers more information about Aristotle, and so on. Let us suppose it is discovered later on that Aristotle was not born in Stagira at all, but in Thebes. We will not now say that the meaning of the name has changed, or that Aristotle did not really exist at all. In short, explaining the use of a name by citing characteristics of the object is not giving the rules for the name, for the rules contain no descriptive content at all. They simply correlate the name to the object independently of any descriptions of it.'

But is the argument convincing? Suppose most or even all of our present factual knowledge of Aristotle proved to be true of no one at all, or of several people living in scattered countries and in different centuries? Would we not say for this reason that Aristotle did not exist after all, and that the name, though it has a conventional sense, refers to no one at all? On the above account, if anyone said that Aristotle did not exist, this must simply be another way of saying that 'Aristotle' denoted no objects, and nothing more; but if anyone did say that Aristotle did not exist he might mean much more than simply that the name does not denote anyone.[1] If, for example, we challenged his statement by pointing out that a man named 'Aristotle' lived in Hoboken in 1903, he would not regard this as a relevant countercharge. We say of Cerberus and Zeus that neither of them ever existed, without meaning that no object ever bore these names, but only that certain kinds (descriptions) of objects never existed and bore these names. So now it looks as though proper names do have a sense necessarily but have a reference only contingently. They begin to look more and more like shorthand and perhaps vague descriptions.

Let us summarize the two conflicting views under consideration: the first asserts that proper names have essentially a reference but not a sense—proper names denote but do not connote; the second asserts that they have essentially a sense and only contingently a reference—they refer only on the condition that one and only one object satisfies their sense.

These two views are paths leading to divergent and hoary metaphysical systems. The first leads to ultimate objects of reference, the substances of the scholastics and the *Gegenstände* of the *Tractatus*. The second leads to the identity of indiscernibles, and variables of quantification as the only referential terms in the language. The subject-predicate structure of the language suggests that the first must be right, but the way we use and teach the use of proper names suggests that it cannot be right: a philosophical problem.

Let us begin by examining the second. If it is asserted that every proper name has a sense, it must be legitimate to demand of any name, 'What is its sense?'. If it is asserted that a proper name is a kind of shorthand description then we ought to be able to present the description in place of the proper name. But how are we to proceed with this? If we try to present a complete description of the object as the sense of a proper name, odd consequences would ensue, e.g. that any true statement about the object using the name as subject would be analytic, any false one self-contradictory, that the meaning of the name (and perhaps the identity of the object)

---

[1] Cf. Wittgenstein, *Philosophical Investigations*, para. 79.

would change every time there was any change at all in the object, that the name would have different meanings for different people, etc. So suppose we ask what are the necessary and sufficient conditions for applying a particular name to a particular object. Suppose for the sake of argument that we have independent means for locating an object; then what are the conditions for applying a name to it; what are the conditions for saying, e.g. 'This is Aristotle'? At first sight these conditions seem to be simply that the object must be identical with an object originally christened by this name, so the sense of the name would consist in a statement or set of statements asserting the characteristics which constitute this identity. The sense of 'This is Aristotle' might be, 'This object is spatio-temporally continuous with an object originally named "Aristotle"'. But this will not suffice, for, as was already suggested, the force of 'Aristotle' is greater than the force of 'identical with an object named "Aristotle"', for not just any object named 'Aristotle' will do. 'Aristotle' here refers to a particular object named 'Aristotle', not to any. 'Named "Aristotle"' is a universal term, but 'Aristotle', is a proper name, so 'This is named "Aristotle"' is at best a necessary but not a sufficient condition for the truth of 'This is Aristotle'. Briefly and trivially, it is not the identity of this with any object named 'Aristotle', but rather its identity with Aristotle that constitutes the necessary and sufficient conditions for the truth of 'This is Aristotle'.

Perhaps we can resolve the conflict between the two views of the nature of proper names by asking what is the unique function of proper names in our language. To begin with, they mostly refer or purport to refer to particular objects; but of course other expressions, definite descriptions and demonstratives, perform this function as well. What then is the difference between proper names and other singular referring expressions? Unlike demonstratives, a proper name refers without presupposing any stage settings or any special contextual conditions surrounding the utterance of the expression. Unlike definite descriptions, they do not in general *specify* any characteristics at all of the objects to which they refer. 'Scott' refers to the same object as does 'the author of *Waverley*', but 'Scott' specifies none of its characteristics, whereas 'the author of *Waverley*' refers only in virtue of the fact that it does specify a characteristic. Let us examine this difference more closely. Following Strawson[1] we may say that referring uses of both proper names and definite

[1] 'On Referring', *Mind* (1950).

descriptions presuppose the existence of one and only one object referred to. But as a proper name does not in general specify any characteristics of the object referred to, how then does it bring the reference off? How is a connexion between name and object ever set up? This, which seems the crucial question, I want to answer by saying that though proper names do not normally assert or specify any characteristics, their referring uses nonetheless presuppose that the object to which they purport to refer has certain characteristics. But which ones? Suppose we ask the users of the name 'Aristotle' to state what they regard as certain essential and established facts about him. Their answers would be a set of uniquely referring descriptive statements. Now what I am arguing is that the descriptive force of 'This is Aristotle' is to assert that a sufficient but so far unspecified number of these statements are true of this object. Therefore, referring uses of 'Aristotle' presuppose the existence of an object of whom a sufficient but so far unspecified number of these statements are true. To use a proper name referringly is to presuppose the truth of certain uniquely referring descriptive statements, but it is not ordinarily to assert these statements or even to indicate which exactly are presupposed. And herein lies most of the difficulty. The question of what constitutes the criteria for 'Aristotle' is generally left open, indeed it seldom in fact arises, and when it does arise it is we, the users of the name, who decide more or less arbitrarily what these criteria shall be. If, for example, of the characteristics agreed to be true of Aristotle, half should be discovered to be true of one man and half true of another, which would we say was Aristotle? Neither? The question is not decided for us in advance.

But is this imprecision as to what characteristics exactly constitute the necessary and sufficient conditions for applying a proper name a mere accident, a product of linguistic slovenliness? Or does it derive from the functions which proper names perform for us? To ask for the criteria for applying the name 'Aristotle' is to ask in the formal mode what Aristotle is; it is to ask for a set of identity criteria for the object Aristotle. 'What is Aristotle?' and 'What are the criteria for applying the name "Aristotle"?' ask the same question, the former in the material mode, and the latter in the formal mode of speech. So if we came to agreement in advance of using the name on precisely what characteristics constituted the identity of Aristotle, our rules for using the name would be precise. But this precision would be achieved only at the cost of entailing some specific predicates by any referring use of the name. Indeed, the name itself would become superfluous for it would become logically equivalent to this set of descriptions. But if this were the case we would be in the position of only being able to refer to an object by describing it. Whereas in fact this is just what the institution of proper names enables us to avoid and what distinguishes proper names from descriptions. If the criteria for proper names were in all cases quite rigid and specific then a proper name would be nothing more than a shorthand for these criteria, a proper name would function exactly like an elaborate definite description. But the uniqueness and immense pragmatic convenience of proper names in our language lie precisely in the fact that they enable us to refer publicly to objects without being forced to raise issues and come to agreement on what descriptive character-istics exactly constitute the identity of the object. They function not as descriptions, but as pegs on which to hang descriptions. Thus the looseness of the criteria for proper names is a necessary condition for isolating the referring function from the describing function of language.

To put the same point differently, suppose we ask. 'Why do we have proper names at all?' Obviously, to refer to individuals. 'Yes, but descriptions could do that for us.' But only at the cost of specify-ing identity conditions every time reference is made: suppose we agree to drop 'Aristotle' and use, say, 'the teacher of Alexander', then it is a necessary truth that the man referred to is Alexander's teacher—but it is a contingent fact that Aristotle ever went into pedagogy (though I am suggesting it is a necessary fact that Aristotle has the logical sum, inclusive disjunction, of properties commonly attributed to him: any individual not having at least some of these properties could not be Aristotle).

Of course it should not be thought that the only sort of looseness of identity criteria for individuals is that which I have described as peculiar to proper names. Referring uses of definite descriptions may raise problems concerning identity of quite different sorts. This is especially true of past tense definite descriptions. 'This is the man who taught Alexander' may be said to entail, e.g. that this object is spatio-temporally continuous with the man teaching Alexander at another point in space-time: but someone might also argue that this man's spatio-temporal continuity is a contingent characteristic and not an identity criterion. And the logical nature of the connexion of such characteristics with the man's identity may again be loose and undecided in advance of dispute. But this is quite another dimension of looseness than that which I cited as the looseness of the criteria for applying proper names and does not affect the distinction in function between definite descriptions and proper names, viz. that definite descriptions refer only in virtue of the fact that the criteria are not loose in the original sense, for they refer by telling us what the object is. But proper names refer without so far raising the issue of what the object is.

We are now in a position to explain how it is that 'Aristotle' has a reference but does not describe, and yet the statement 'Aristotle never existed' says more than that 'Aristotle' was never used to refer to any object. The statement asserts that a sufficient number of the conventional presuppositions, descriptive statements, of referring uses of 'Aristotle' are false. Precisely which statements are asserted to be false is not yet clear, for what precise conditions constitute the criteria for applying 'Aristotle' is not yet laid down by the language.

We can now resolve our paradox: does a proper name have a sense? If this asks whether or not proper names are used to describe or specify characteristics of objects, the answer is 'no'. But if it asks whether or not proper names are logically connected with characteristics of the object to which they refer, the answer is 'yes, in a loose sort of way'. (This shows in part the poverty of a rigid sense-reference, denotation-connotation approach to problems in the theory of meaning.)

We might clarify these points by comparing paradigmatic proper names with degenerate proper names like 'The Bank of England'. For these latter, it seems the sense is given as straightforwardly as in a definite description; the presuppositions, as it were, rise to the surface. And a proper name may acquire a rigid descriptive use without having the verbal form of a description: God is just, omnipotent, omniscient, etc., *by definition* for believers. Of course the form may mislead us; the Holy Roman Empire was neither holy, nor Roman, etc., but it was nonetheless the Holy Roman Empire. Again it may be conventional to name only girls 'Martha', but if I name my son 'Martha' I may mislead, but I do not lie.

Now reconsider our original identity, 'Tully = Cicero'. A statement made using this sentence would, I suggest, be analytic for most people; the same descriptive presuppositions are associated with each name. But of course if the descriptive presuppositions were different it might be used to make a synthetic statement; it might even advance a historical discovery of the first importance.

VI

IS EXISTENCE A PREDICATE?

(1) D. F. PEARS

IT is impossible to answer the question whether existence is a predicate or not before we know what the question means. What would be meant by a philosopher who said, as many do say, that existence is not a predicate?

The first point that I want to make is that some of the formulations of the thesis that existence is not a predicate are too inexact to be much help. For instance, it is sometimes said that, if I assert that tigers exist, the verb 'exist' does not add anything to the concept of the subject 'tigers'. But there is a sense in which this is false: for to say that a concept has instances in reality is certainly to add something to it, even if what is added is peculiar. And it *is* peculiar, because it is unlike what is added to the concept 'tiger' when I assert that tigers are striped. But the peculiarity of what is added when I assert that tigers exist does not justify the conclusion that nothing is added. Consequently this formulation of the thesis that existence is not a predicate will need to be refined. It is too inexact to say simply that the verb 'exists' adds nothing to the concept of the subject.

Similarly it is too inexact to say that the thesis means that when I assert that tigers exist, I am not saying anything about tigers. For this too is, in one sense, false, since anyone who was asked what I was talking about could answer quite correctly 'tigers'. And it would be equally correct for him to give this answer even if I had said 'Tigers do not exist'; or—to change the example to a true negative existential statement—if I had said 'Griffins do not exist', it would have been equally correct for him to say that this was about griffins. So this formulation of the thesis that existence is not a predicate will also need to be refined. It is too inexact to say simply that an existential statement is not about the subject; e.g., not about tigers or not about griffins.

What I shall do now is to take these inexact formulations of the

Aquinas Paper 38 (Aquin Press, 1963). © Aquin Press, 1963. Reprinted, with minor alterations to his paper by D. F. Pears, by permission of the authors and the Aquin Press.

thesis and refine them. My aim in refining them will be to extract a minimal formulation of the thesis that existence is not a predicate; i.e., to extract a formulation that is at least part of what people have meant by the thesis. I shall do this in two stages, first considering singular existential statements and then considering general existential statements.

First suppose that I make the singular existential statement 'This room exists'. Clearly there is something very odd about this statement. For the subject-phrase 'This room' implies that this room exists by making a reference to it, and the verb 'exists' asserts its existence all over again. Thus the verb 'exists' is redundant. Of course not all uses of the word 'this' produce this result. But when, as in this case, it is used to refer to something in the speaker's environment, it does make the verb 'exist' redundant, and so the whole statement might be called a 'referential tautology'. Now suppose that I say instead 'This room does not exist'; then this statement will be a referential contradiction since, like the affirmative version, it implies, simply by its reference, that the room exists, and then, unlike the affirmative version, it goes on to deny its existence with the verb 'does not exist', and this is a contradiction.

Now these two ideas—referential tautology and referential contradiction—are really refinements of the ideas used in the two inexact formulations of the thesis that existence is not a predicate. For we get a referential tautology when the statement refers to the thing that it is about in such a way that it implies its existence, so that the verb 'exists' adds nothing new. Conversely, if the verb were 'does not exist' it would be trying to subtract what had already been referentially implied, and this would produce a referential contradiction. So we have now extracted the point from the two inexact versions—that the verb 'exists' adds nothing, and that existential statements are not about their subjects. 'Adds nothing' means 'adds nothing new', and 'being about something' means 'being about something in such a way that its existence is referentially implied'.

So perhaps we could say that the thesis that existence is not a predicate at least means that the verb 'to exist' produces referential tautologies and referential contradictions in this way. This is the minimal formulation, which is at least part of what has been meant by the thesis. It could, of course, be expressed equally well by saying that if existence is a predicate, it is a peculiar predicate. But probably all formulations of the thesis would allow this weaker form of expression.

The minimal formulation that I have just given will not do as it stands. For it needs to be qualified in at least three ways.

First, it might happen that the subject-phrase of a singular existential statement referred to something or somebody in the world of fiction, and so implied existence in that world, but did not imply existence in the real world. For instance, I might refer to a character in 'The Remembrance of Things Past' and say that he existed in real life. If I did this, the subject-phrase of my statement—the name of the character—would imply existence only in the world created by Proust, and consequently, when I went on to assert that the person also existed in real life I would be adding something new. So my statement would not be a referential tautology. The reason for this is plain: the statement would have a connexion with two worlds; it would imply existence in the world of fiction and assert existence in the real world. And if my statement had denied existence in the real world instead of asserting it, it would have avoided being a referential contradiction in the same way.

Secondly, there is another similar qualification of the minimal formulation that has to be made. Suppose that I say 'The Euston Arch no longer exists'. Since the subject of this statement referentially implies existence in the real world, and since the verb denies existence in the real world it might look as if this statement is a referential contradiction. But in fact it is not. For existence in the real world is implied at one time and denied at another time, and in this way a referential contradiction is avoided. Similarly, if the statement had been affirmative, it would have avoided being a referential tautology. General existential statements produce a parallel phenomenon: e.g., the statement 'Dodos are extinct'.

The third qualification is more difficult to characterize precisely. Suppose that I see a dagger and have good reason to believe that it is only an hallucination. Then I might say 'That dagger does not exist'. How does this statement avoid being a referential contradiction? For there is no doubt that it does *somehow* escape contradiction. Here, I think, we need to make a distinction between two different aspects under which the dagger might be considered to exist. First, it might exist as a visually experienced dagger, and the subject phrase 'That dagger' referentially implies that it exists *at least* on that level. But, secondly, it might exist as a dagger in space, and the verb 'does not exist' denies that it exists on that level. The result is that there is no incompatibility between what is implied and what is denied. And if the statement had been affirmative—'That dagger exists'—the verb would have added something new. Mirages, ghosts, and other kinds of sensory replica could be treated in a similar way.

This third qualification does not depend on a difference in time, like the second one. Nor does it depend on a distinction between the world of fiction and the real world, like the first one. For, though the phenomenological world which contains hallucinations differs from the real world of things in space, it is not the same as the world of fiction. Fiction is deliberately invented by us, but hallucinations happen to us.

When the qualifications have been added to the original minimal formulation, we have the following thesis: If the subject-phrase of a singular statement referentially implies existence, then, if the verb asserts existence, the statement will be a referential tautology, and, if the verb denies existence, the statement will be a referential contradiction, except under one of the following three conditions—first, the implication and the assertion are about different worlds; secondly they are about different times; thirdly they are about different levels.

This thesis could be refined still further. For there would probably turn out to be further exceptions to it if we searched carefully for them. And the thesis suffers from the weakness that it relies on the unanalysed notion of reference. Still, I think that it may serve as a fairly close minimal formulation of what has been meant by those who have denied that existence is a predicate. And this minimal formulation seems to be true. Of course, as I said earlier, it could be expressed equally well by saying that existence is a peculiar kind of predicate. But the important thing is the truth behind the thesis, rather than the actual words in which it is epigrammatically expressed.

At this point it would be possible to broaden the topic by asking what other predicates are peculiar in the same way, or in a similar way. The predicates 'possible', 'probable' and 'necessary' would suggest themselves as candidates for investigation. But I am not going to follow up this line of thought. Instead I shall say something about general existential statements.

In what I have been saying about singular existential statements I have been following up some ideas that G. E. Moore put forward in his article 'Is Existence a Predicate?'.[1] When Moore examined general existential statements in that article he pointed out, among other things, that there is a difference between the two statements 'All tame

[1] *Proceedings of the Aristotelian Society*, Supp. Vol. (1963).

tigers growl' and 'All tame tigers exist'. The second statement in this pair is, of course, a general existential statement, whereas the first is general but not existential. But the interesting thing is, that though the first statement is all right, the second lacks a clear sense. Can we appeal to the minimal formulation in order to explain this difference? I think that we can, in the following way: The phrase 'All tame tigers' here referentially implies that there exist tame tigers in the real world. Consequently it is a referential tautology to go on to assert that they exist. And if I had gone on to deny that they exist, that would have been a referential contradiction. For what non-contradictory sense could be given to the statement 'All tame tigers are non-existent'? There would seem to be only one way of giving it a sense, and that is to invoke the first qualification of the minimal formulation, and to say that it refers to tame tigers in works of fiction that may or may not have been taken from real life. But that is such a tortuous expedient that it justifies us in saying that the statement lacks a clear sense. Contrast Moore's other statement—'All tame tigers growl' where the verb 'growl', unlike the verb 'exist', adds something new, which could therefore be subtracted without contradiction.

Moore also examined another pair of statements—'Some tame tigers growl' and 'Some tame tigers exist'. Both of these make perfectly good sense. But there is a striking difference between them. For we can add to the first one the words 'and some do not', whereas, if we add this supplement to the second one, the result is a kind of nonsense. Can we again appeal to the minimal formulation in order to explain this difference? I think that it is possible to do so in the following way: If I say 'Some tame tigers growl and some do not', I am referentially implying that there exist tame tigers in the real world, and I am dividing them into two classes, those that possess the predicate 'growler', and those that do not. And this is perfectly all right. But if I say 'Some tame tigers exist and some do not' it sounds as if I am doing the same sort of thing. But I cannot be, since if I were, half of what I was asserting would be a referential tautology, and half a referential contradiction. Again it would be a desperate expedient to invoke the second qualification of the minimal formulation in order to give my extraordinary assertion a sense.

So it is possible to extend the minimal formulation to cover general existential statements. But, as I said earlier, the minimal formulation suffers from the weakness that it depends on the unanalysed notion of reference. How do we know when a subject-phrase makes a reference? I assumed that a reference was being made by the phrase 'Some tame tigers' in the extraordinary assertion that I have just been discussing. But in the statement 'Some tame tigers exist' it clearly does not make a reference since this is not a referential tautology. Similarly 'the king of France' may make a reference in the statement 'The king of France is bald' but it certainly does not make a reference in the statement 'The king of France does not exist'. These anomalies could be dealt with inside the framework of the minimal formulation. But they suggest another, different possibility, which is to abandon the notion of reference, and to treat existence in the way that Russell treated it.

'Existence gives rise to referential tautology and referential contradiction. So it is different from most predicates, and if we wish
to classify it as a predicate we must be prepared to regard it as a
peculiar one.' Mr Pears suggests this as a cautious reformulation of
the old idea that existence is not a predicate. As he himself says, the
reformulated thesis leaves it open that existence is a predicate, after
all. So it might be better to speak of the reason behind the traditional
denial, rather than of a reformulation of it. But this is not really
important. The question is whether there are other reasons for the
denial which are more clearly conclusive, and, if there are not, why
some logicians insist on the stronger way of putting the matter.

Let us first make a distinction. A predicate is a certain type of word
or phrase, such as 'runs', 'is warm', 'is not warm', 'is married to
the younger sister of a violinist'. Then, whatever *existence* may be,
it is certainly not a predicate, since it is not a word or a phrase. So
then, it may seem that the question must be 'Is (the verb) "exists"
a predicate?' That is how Mr Pears tacitly takes it. And if that is the
question, then there seems no reason for not returning an affirmative
answer.

But this is not the only way of taking the original question. Instead
of taking our cue from the word 'predicate', and supplying a suitable
subject for the question, we could instead take our cue from the
world 'existence' and ask something about *it*. The question would
then be whether existence, the 'thing' now, if it is even a 'thing', is
an *attribute*. Suppose I say that $\sqrt{2}$ exists, at least in the space of real
numbers, do I attribute existence to $\sqrt{2}$? You will see that we at once
come up against Mr Pears' difficulty. For it is natural to feel that I can
attribute existence to $\sqrt{2}$ only because it is, so to speak, there for me
to attribute something to it.

It may be objected all the same that there is no difference between
the two questions, that they come to the same thing. Isn't the second
just a 'material mode' statement of the first? The answer to this is
that there are more *semantic controls* on the word 'predicate' than
there are on the word 'attribute'. Grammar books sometimes give
rules for parsing sentences, and these rules and rules of that general
type are investigated by the new mathematical linguists. According
to the old rules, 'exists' is certainly a predicate. A schoolboy would
be expected to parse Mr Pears' example-sentence. 'This room exists'
in the same way as he would parse 'This room is pleasantly warm'.

And it is very plausible that any fairly simple and workable theory of syntax and sentence-construction would have the same consequence. So, not only is there no reason for denying that 'exists' is a predicate, but there is a positive reason for not doing so.

But we must now notice that the logicians who say that 'exists' isn't a predicate would not deny any of this. Yes, they would say, it is a *grammatical predicate*, but it isn't a *logical one*. And indeed, they might add, it is just because it is a grammatical predicate that we are anxious to deny that it is a logical one. For its being the first makes people take for granted that it is the second too, and then horrible confusions and misunderstandings result.

Now if what I suggested a moment ago was correct, the notion of a predicate *belongs anyway* to grammar, or to its new and smart descendant, syntax. But then, it would seem, there is no question of 'exists' being grammatically a predicate and logically something else. What then is meant by saying that it isn't a logical predicate?

I shall here cut short this part of the discussion and say at once what I think the answer to this question is: by a 'logical predicate' is meant something that would be a predicate in an interpretation of predicate-logic, i.e., what is sometimes called functional logic of first order, or again first-order quantification theory. In this logic, we have name-signs, such as a, b, c, ..., variables, x, y, z ... predicate-letters, F, G, H, ..., and quantifiers and truth-functional operators. Then among the formulas constructed from these primitive materials there are

Fa, Gab, (Ex) Fx, (Ex) Gxa, (x) (Ey) Gxy,

and these can be regarded as representing or depicting the logical form (or better, perhaps, a logical form) of such statements as, respectively,

John is happy. Room 101 is warm. 2 is prime;

John loves Mary. Room 101 is warmer than Room 102. 2 divides 16.

Someone loves John. At least one number divides 16.

Everyone loves someone or other. Every number is a divisor.

The formation-rules of predicate-logic supply a very simple theory of the syntax (grammar) of enormously many everyday statements. It follows that they can be regarded also as supplying the *whole* theory of the syntax of a language which is like English but poorer than it, and hence simpler than it. With respect to such a language, predicates would be distinguished in a very simple and satisfactory way. Every sentence in the language would be obtainable from a formula of predicate-logic by some one or more of a fixed set of substitutions

And the question whether such and such a phrase in a sentence was a predicate would be answered simply by seeing whether that phrase had been got by substitution on a predicate-letter. (Notice that this is not circular; I explained what signs in the formalism were to be called 'predicate-letters' before I said what their role was to be; I could equally well have spoken of P-letters, or signs of the third kind, or something like that.) For such a language, then, and such a theory of its syntax, the question what phrases were predicates would not be a question requiring thought or reflection, but could be determined, at least in principle, in a purely mechanical way.

I want now to suggest that the idea of a *logical* predicate is not the idea of a special sort of predicate, nor a special or 'logical' idea of a predicate, but is the ordinary (grammatical) idea of a predicate, with respect, however, to a special language. And that when logicians say that 'exists', or existence, is not a logical predicate, what they mean is that it is not treated as one in first-order predicate-logic (i.e., it would not be a predicate at all in the simple language I envisaged).

We have now arrived at another cautious and exact thesis to replace the old idea that existence is not a predicate. How important is that thesis? Is it an interesting one?

What makes the thesis at least worth noticing is a set of facts about the new and simple language envisaged. For it seems that for practically any serious statement which we might want to make containing the word 'exists', we can find a statement in the new language which would serve the same purpose and would not contain the word 'exists' at all. The reasons for saying that 'exists' is not a (logical) predicate come down, then, to saying that though 'exists' is a predicate it is a dispensable one. We do utter sentences in which 'exists' occurs as a predicate; but we have no need to do so. For example, instead of saying that the round square does not exist, we can say instead that no square is round, or that, whatever figure you care to take, that figure will not be both square and round. For existence-statements containing proper names in a certain way, such as 'Homer did not really exist' we may need to imagine our language supplied with a certain amount of 'theory', e.g., about Homer; this is tantamount to saying that we must allow the translation of 'Homer did not exist' to be governed by beliefs about Homer, so that the translation might be that no one wrote both the Odyssey and the Iliad. But perhaps this is reasonable enough.

At the end of his paper, Mr Pears mentioned briefly a more ambitious thesis than the one he was himself proposing, and mentioned Lord Russell in this connexion. It is of course Russell's theory that I have, with many qualifications, been explaining. Russell says that a sentence like 'The round square does not exist' is misleading as to the logical form of the fact expressed by it. If we ask here what is the logical form of the fact involved, we shall be referred to the translation of the statement already mentioned. What is difficult here is the idea of being able to identify the logical form of a fact independently of the grammatical form of some sentence which states it. The relation between sentence and fact is not like that between a picture and the thing depicted, where we can look from picture to model and so assess the picture as a likeness. And I think this means that in saying that a sentence S is misleading because of its form, we can only be claiming that some other sentence, S' which in some sense says the same thing but says it differently, is preferable. But this does not mean that the whole idea of logical translation becomes silly. For the preferred sentence really may be preferable. The logical relations of the assertion that unicorns do not exist are probably better grasped through the sentence 'No animal is a unicorn' than they are through the sentence 'Unicorns do not exist'. But it remains the case that we could not hope to show by this kind of method that 'exists' isn't a predicate. The translation-technique could only seem to show such a thing if it were thought that some special status could be claimed for predicate-logic.

THE *A PRIORI* AND THE ANALYTIC

I

THERE is something unsatisfactory about the way in which the doctrine that all *a priori* statements are analytic—I shall call it the analytic thesis for convenience—is ordinarily defended. In its great days, thirty years ago, its opponents would ask: what is the status of the thesis itself? It is not empirical, but it does not appear to be analytic either. Therefore it is a refutation of itself. Those of its defenders who did not take refuge behind the insecure defence of the theory of types, admitting that it was *a priori*, insisted that it was, despite appearances, analytic. But they did not treat it as if it were. Instead of attempting to prove it they put it forward more as an hypothesis, supporting it with representative pieces of favourable evidence and attempting to dispose of apparent counter-examples. In practice controversy settled, or bogged, down around a handful of particular cases: for example, 'nothing can be red and green all over' and the transitivity of 'earlier than'.

If the thesis is analytic this kind of inductive argument is misplaced. Examples may suggest an analytic generalization in the first place and be used to illustrate and clarify it, to make the theoretical arguments for it more concrete and intelligible, but they cannot establish it. It was a bad habit of Moore's to base conceptual truths on particular instances. In his attack on naturalism he inferred that 'good' was different in meaning from any natural or descriptive term whatever from the application of a dubious technique of conceptual intuition to a few selected instances of naturalistic definition. No proof or explanation of the general differences between the ethical and the non-ethical was offered. In the same way he concluded that 'exists' was not a predicate from some particular differences of logical behaviour between it and some ordinary predicates.

From *Proceedings of the Aristotelian Society*, Vol. 64 (1963-4), pp. 31-54. Reprinted by courtesy of the author and the Editor of the Aristotelian Society.

How should *a priori* truths be established? Something like the traditional view that *a priori* knowledge rests on intuition or demonstration must be correct. *A priori* truths must be established either directly or by deduction from those that have been. They must be seen or shown to be true. If any are to be demonstrated some must be intuited as self-evident in order to halt the regress of demonstration by providing ultimate premises and to supply the rules of inference that are applied to them. The discovery that a body of *a priori* truths can be deduced equally well from distinct sets of axioms has brought this notion of logical intuition into disfavour. But it does not follow from the fact that there is no unique set of formally sufficient axioms, complete, consistent and independent, that there is no question of material adequacy. It is one thing for the theorems of a system to follow from its axioms, another for either of them to be acceptable as true. Axioms only confer truth on theorems if they are true themselves. A formally sufficient axiom will be materially adequate only if it is intuitive. According to the analytic thesis, an *a priori* truth is intuitive if its acceptance as true is a condition of understanding the terms it contains.

It is fairly clear that the analytic thesis is not intuitive. The fact of controversy about the thesis is not quite conclusive since it is abstractly possible that the defenders of the thesis attach a different sense to the term 'analytic' from the sense or senses ascribed by its opponents, one in which 'analytic' and '*a priori*' are bare synonyms. If this were the case it could not go undetected for it would be the only way in which defenders of the thesis, taking it to be intuitive, could account for the obvious fact of hostility to it. The fact that there are familiar explicit definitions of the crucial terms involved, in none of which is either term straightforwardly defined by reference to the other, shows that this general misunderstanding does not obtain in practice. '*A priori*' means either, widely, 'non-empirical' or, narrowly, following Kant, 'necessary'. To assimilate these is to make the questionable assumption that all non-empirical truths are necessary which I shall discuss later. 'Analytic', I would suggest, has had four main interpretations. (i) In the first and widest, an analytic statement is one true in virtue of the meaning of the terms it contains. (ii) As understood by Leibniz and Kant, an analytic statement is a tautology that repeats itself, asserts no more than it assumes, is an instance of the law of identity whose denial is an explicit contradiction. (iii) As understood by those who take Hobbes's view of necessary truth, an analytic statement is one that is true in virtue of the conventions of language.

(iv) Finally, as understood by Frege and most modern logicians, an analytic statement is a truth of logic or reducible to one with the help of definitions. The identity of these four definitions of 'analytic' with the two definitions of '*a priori*' is not intuitively obvious, nor is their identity with each other. In this paper I propose to argue, first, that all *necessary a priori* truths are analytic in the first and widest sense and then, building on this conclusion, which is not itself contentious, that such truths are also analytic in the other three senses. And for each of the four identifications involved I shall offer a general argument.

II

I shall begin with a proof of the analytic thesis in the widest interpretation of the two crucial terms involved: that all non-empirical statements are true (or false) in virtue of their meaning. I hasten to admit that it will seem disappointingly trivial. I shall also consider an objection which, by casting doubt on one side of the thesis in this form without, however, touching the essentials of the thesis, provides a good reason for interpreting it in accordance with the narrower, Kantian sense of '*a priori*' as: all necessary statements are true (or false) in virtue of their meaning. For convenience of exposition I shall speak only of true statements hereafter but the adjustments required to include false statements are obvious.

The proof starts from the commonplace distinction between necessary and contingent statements. A necessary truth is one that is true in itself, true, in Lewis's phrase, 'no matter what', must be true and cannot be false. A contingent truth, as etymology suggests, is one that is true dependently on or because of something else, something outside itself. As depending on this something else it does not have to be true. The necessary and the contingent make an exclusive and exhaustive division of the realm of truths. I shall argue that the correlated distinctions of the analytic from the synthetic and of the *a priori* from the empirical coincide with the distinction of the necessary from the contingent since they both arise from elucidations of one of the none too sharply defined elements of that distinction.

To start with the distinction of analytic and synthetic. Here 'analytic' is the positive element. It is a development or elucidation of the idea of the necessary. If a truth is necessary it is true in itself and independently of everything outside it. The statement itself consists of a form of words with a meaning attached. But it is not the form of words that determines the truth of the statement. If 'lie' is defined as 'false statement made with intent to deceive' the words 'every lie is a falsehood' express a necessary truth but if 'lie' is defined as 'statement believed false made with intent to deceive' then they express a contingent falsehood. Since there is nothing more to the statement than the words it is composed of and the meaning they are given and since the words do not determine its truth, if it is true in itself it must be true in virtue of its meaning.

In the *a priori*-empirical distinction the positive element is 'empirical'. The term '*a priori*' just sweeps up the residue of non-empirical truths. The idea of the empirical is a development or elucidation of the idea of the contingent. It aims to explain how a statement can owe its truth to something else, what conditions the something else must satisfy if it is to confer truth on a statement. To require it to be experience is to say that unless it is something of whose existence we can in principle become aware then the form of words involved has not made out its claim to be a statement. No limit is set here to the possible forms of experience or awareness, in particular no equation of experience and sense-experience is implied. For a form of words to be understood as a statement we must know what its truth-conditions are and to know this is to be able to recognize them when they occur, to know what it would be like to experience them.

If these arguments are correct all and only necessary truths are analytic and all and only contingent truths are empirical. Since necessary and contingent truths are exclusive no truth is *both* analytic *and* empirical, since they are exhaustive every truth is *either* analytic *or* empirical. Since 'synthetic' means 'non-analytic' and '*a priori*' means 'non-empirical' every truth is synthetic or *a priori* and no truth is both.

This excessively tidy-looking argument explains why there should be many defenders of synthetic *a priori* truths but none for analytic empirical truths. 'Analytic' and 'empirical' are both positively defined. If a statement is analytic it is true in virtue of its meaning, if empirical in virtue of experience. But if it is true in virtue of its meaning there is no room left for experience to have any effect on it and if it is true in virtue of experience then its meaning cannot have been sufficient to determine its truth. The synthetic and the *a priori*, on the other hand, are defined negatively, by exclusion. If a statement is synthetic it does not owe its truth to its meaning, if *a priori* not to experience. But might it not owe its truth to some third consideration beyond both of them? If, as I have argued, the analytic and the empirical are simply elucidations of the exhaustive concepts of the necessary and the contingent there is no third possibility. Meaning and experience must be as exhaustive as the two concepts they are used to explain.

One part of the analytic thesis in the interpretation we are considering, its claim that all contingent statements are empirical, has recently been challenged in a way that does not touch the main point at issue and enables it to be more sharply defined. Watkins, following Popper, has argued that statements which are both universally and existentially quantified, like 'every event has a cause' and 'every metal has a solvent', are neither analytic nor empirical. He points out that an important class of metaphysical propositions are of this form and are, therefore, synthetic *a priori*. They are not empirical, he maintains, because, like all unrestricted existential statements, they cannot be conclusively falsified. So far we have taken an empirical statement to be one that is true (or false) in virtue of experience. But this is not clear. We can interpret 'empirical' strongly, as 'conclusively verifiable or falsifiable by experience', or weakly, as 'confirmable or disconfirmable by experience'. Popper chooses a definition falling between these extremes for two main reasons. First, science consists mainly of universal statements which are essential for explanation and prediction. The only existential statements it contains are restricted or circumscribed, asserting that something of a certain sort exists, not at some unspecified place and time, but in a circumscribed spatio-temporal region, and such statements can be falsified. Secondly, an empirical statement is one that can be empirically tested and to test something is to see how much it can stand, to see whether it can be destroyed. So the empirical test of a statement is its exposure to the possibility of refutation, of conclusive falsification. That which cannot in principle be refuted cannot be seriously tested.

If we accept conclusive falsifiability by experience as a criterion of the empirical it follows that all unrestricted existential statements are non-empirical. But such statements are ordinarily synthetic so they are synthetic *a priori* in the wide sense of the latter term. But it is important to notice that they are also contingent. They are not *a priori* in the strong, Kantian sense that implies necessity. It is only because of the hold of Kant's identification of the *a priori* with the necessary that this defence of the synthetic *a priori* seems at first sight to conflict with the analytic thesis. What emerges is that the essential content of the thesis is that all *necessary* truths are analytic.

Now if this is taken to mean, in accordance with the first and widest definition of 'analytic', that all necessary truths are true in virtue of the meaning of the terms they contain it will be objected, not that it is false, but that it lacks substance. Certainly most of the leading defenders of the synthetic *a priori* agree that necessary truths owe their truth to their meaning. In *The Problems Of Philosophy*, Russell says, "all *a priori* knowledge deals exclusively with the relations of universals" (p. 103). Since universals are at any rate the meanings of general terms this amounts to an acceptance of the present form of the thesis. Broad says that an *a priori* proposition is either one that can be seen to be true "by merely inspecting it and reflecting on its terms and their mode of combination" or else the logical consequence of such a proposition (*P.A.S. Supp. Vol.* 15 (1936), p. 102). Ewing says that the truth of an *a priori* proposition "depends wholly on the meaning of the terms used" (*P.A.S.*, 1939–40, p. 231). Kneale, finally, says that "anything we come to know *a priori* . . . is learnt by reflection on the meanings of words or other symbols" (*The Development Of Logic*, p. 636). Pap sums the matter up in a criticism of C. I. Lewis. "The term 'analytic' is sometimes used in the strict sense of demonstrability on the basis of definitions and principles of logic, sometimes in a broader sense which is often expressed as 'certifiable as true by reflection upon meanings alone' . . . The broader sense of 'analytic' is not distinguishable at all from the sense of '*a priori*', so that by this interpretation the empiricist thesis is true but trivial" (*Semantics And Necessary Truth*, p. 89).

This cloud of witnesses shows that no philosopher who has seriously considered the question is prepared to dispute the view that necessary truth is determined by meaning. But this is not the same thing as triviality. Since I hold that 'necessary' and 'analytic' are demonstrably the same in meaning I am, of course, committed to the position that these concepts are, in the end, indistinguishable. But this is not to say that they are trivially indistinguishable. The definitions of the two terms are not verbally identical and a simple argument is needed to make the step from one to the other. 'Analytic' as 'true in virtue of meaning' gives a little more clarity of outline to the relatively amorphous notion of the necessary as that which is true in itself, no matter what. My witnesses are content to assert that necessary truth depends on meaning without giving reasons for doing so.

The main result of the glimpses into the obvious we have taken so far is that the issue between the defenders and the opponents of the analytic thesis is now more precisely identified. Its defenders believe that necessary truths are also analytic in some or all of the other three senses enumerated at the end of the first section and these further interpretations of the thesis are rejected by its opponents. I shall argue not merely that the three principles embodied in these interpretations, that necessary truths are identities, are true by convention and are reducible to truths of logic, are in fact correct, but that they follow from the first and widest version of the analytic thesis we have so far been dealing with. The three principles are not obviously equivalent for there is no obvious absurdity in accepting some and rejecting the others. I accept all three of them, though the third only with certain qualifications. In each case I shall argue that the principle is a consequence of the original, most inclusive and generally accepted form of the thesis.

III

The principle that necessary truth depends on identity or repetition is a natural development of the thesis that necessity depends on meaning. The claim that we discover the necessary truth of a statement by reflecting on the meaning of its terms, though helpful in a preliminary way, is more suggestive than explanatory. What are we supposed to look for in this process of reflection? How can meanings be so related or connected in a statement that its falsity is ruled out and its truth, therefore, certified?

The answer proposed by the Leibnizian principle rests on a general account of the nature of statements as containing two sorts of factor—I shall call them the assumption and the assertion—which generalizes the familiar idea that every statement contains a subject or referring element and a predicate or describing element. This duality has two different forms. The first is categorical. In a categorical statement 'S is P' to utter the subject-expression 'S' is to assume the existence of what it refers to. The statement then goes on to assert the predicate 'P' of the S that has been assumed to exist. The second form of the duality is hypothetical. In an hypothetical statement 'if p then q', the antecedent makes the hypothetical supposition that the fact obtains which 'p' by itself could be used to state categorically. A categorical necessary truth, then, according to this principle, is of the form 'the F is F' and an hypothetical necessary statement is of the form 'if p then p'. In either case denial involves contradiction: 'the F is not F' and 'p and not-p'.

The question was: how can the meaning of a statement be such as to rule out the possibility of its falsehood and thus make it necessarily true? The reply is that if a statement makes some assumption, categorical or hypothetical, as to how things are and then does no more than assert all or part of what has been thus assumed it runs no risk of falsification. The only way to guarantee that what a statement asserts is correct is to assume that it is. Unless the occurrence of something incompatible with what is asserted is ruled out by the assumption of the statement the assertion may turn out to be false. Necessary truth, then, depends on repetition.

There will be no objection to the claim that if a statement asserts no more than it assumes it is necessarily true. It is the converse claim that is controversial. Unfortunately those who reject it give no clear account of the relation between meanings other than identity they have in mind. The obscurity of their position is compounded by the fact that they are not explicit about how identity succeeds in rendering necessary the statements whose elements' meanings it relates, though they usually agree that it does. Blanshard, for example, says that "elements really different may be intelligibly connected" (*The Nature Of Thought*, Vol. II, p. 408). Certainly elements that are verbally different may be identical in meaning. And elements that differ in meaning may be intelligibly connected in the sense that a reason can be given for the fact that one applies to everything to which the other applies. But these admissions are consistent with the Leibnizian principle. In the first, necessity remains grounded in identity of meaning; in the second, the 'intelligible connexion' is not an identity of meaning but it is not a necessary connexion either.

Underlying these protests on behalf of a non-identical connexion of meanings there seems to be a vivid but unacceptable picture of the Platonic realm of meanings or essences in which they are conceived as being related in as many different ways as are particulars in space and time. To oppose this picture is not to call in question the propriety of conceiving meanings as objects existing in a realm of their own. It is only to insist that if this conception, or way of speaking, is adopted its use should be guided by the actual nature of the things so conceived and not irrelevantly proliferated by unfounded analogies with a more familiar order of things. Meanings, conceived as objects, are not in time or space. It is only through their relations to the devices men have used to express them that they come to have any relations other than identity, total or partial, and distinctness.

We can examine the question at a less breathlessly abstract level by considering a distinction drawn by Ewing between two senses in which the conclusion of a valid deductive inference can be contained in its premises. It may be contained as a part, the position of the

Leibnizian principle, or as merely being entailed by them. As an example of this substantial variety of entailment that does not rest on identity he offers the entailment of q by the conjunction of p and if p then q. Certainly the categorical assertion of q is not explicitly present in the premises. Nor is the joint assertion of the premises together with the negation of the conclusion explicitly self-contradictory. But we can easily turn it into an explicit self-contradiction by substituting 'not (p and not-q)' for 'if p then q' in the formula '(if p then q) and p and not-q'. The same operation can be applied to more complicated laws, for example the truth-functional law of the transitivity of implication.

The ultimate reason for saying that identity is the relation between meanings that gives rise to necessary truth is that identity and its opposite are the only relations that meanings, considered in themselves, can have. The principle that necessity rests on identity of meaning does not strictly entail the position that all necessary truth is categorical or hypothetical. But since I do not see how identity of meaning could make statements necessarily true in any other way I must take serious account of the objection that there are necessary truths which are not of these logical forms.

Two possible examples are easy to deal with. Mathematical equations can be represented as biconditionals about classes or sets: thus '$5 + 7 = 12$' means the same as 'all and only sets with $5 + 7$ members have 12 members'. Negative existential statements like 'there are no round squares' can be understood as hypothetical statements with a negative consequent: 'if anything is round it is not square'. Affirmative existential statements are more troublesome. I would suggest that 'there is a prime number between 5 and 11' can only be established as a consequence of the more specific statement '7 is prime and between 5 and 11' whose three constituents, '7 is prime', '7 is greater than 5' and '7 is less than 11' can be dealt with along the lines suggested for '$5 + 7 = 12$'.

IV

The argument to show that necessary truth is a matter of convention is very simple. A statement is a necessary truth because of the meaning of the words of which it is composed. The meaning that words have is assigned to them by convention. Therefore it is linguistic convention that makes a form of words express a necessary truth. This Hobbesian view makes necessity unmysterious by treating it, not as something objectively discoverable in the nature of things, but as a matter of human decision. The impossibility of falsification that is characteristic of necessary truths is not a brute ontological fact; it is brought about by our refusal from the start to let any falsification occur.

But this simplicity is not to all tastes. Many who know the difficulty of mathematical work from direct experience resent what they take as an insult to mathematicians. We do not decide that

$$x = \frac{-b \pm \sqrt{b^2 - 4ac}}{2a} \text{ if } ax^2 + bx + c = o;$$ we find it out, if we have

the skill, after heavy labour. The theorems of mathematics are discoveries not arbitrary whims. The view that mathematical propositions are tautologies with its apparent implication that they are obvious evokes a similar emotion. Kneale observes, with barely concealed indignation, that Leibniz knew too much about mathematics to regard it as conventional (*op.cit.*, p. 312). But he did not, it seems, know enough about it to realize that its propositions were not identities.

In fact neither of these offensive implications follows from the principles in question. The two equations in the last paragraph are identical in meaning as can readily be shown by substituting the value given for x in the first for the occurrences of x in the second. This is mildly laborious but not difficult. What is hard is to discover the identity in the first place. But an identity is none the less an identity for being deeply hidden. Similarly, the view that necessary truth is conventional does not trivialize it. Kneale's argument about mathematics could just as well be applied to chess to show that its rules are not conventional. To say that it is a game is not to assimilate it to the activity of a child idly kicking a stone along a road.

It follows from the principle that necessity is conventional that the conventions actually in force could have been different from what they are. The fact that the meanings of many non-logical words have changed in the course of time enforces a general agreement that the rules governing them are alterable. But, it is claimed, there is a limit to this alterability. Some hold that no logical law can be replaced by some other rule for the use of logical words. Others, more cautiously, regard the law of contradiction, at least, as indispensable.

The existence of alternative logics with no law of excluded middle is a difficulty for the wider view about the limits of convention. The defence that such systems are only called logics by courtesy, because of their formal analogies to classical logic, is too like obscurantist resistances to non-Euclidean geometry to be very convincing. But there is a sense in which the law of contradiction is unalterable. For no system that rejected it could be used as a logic, a system of the general rules of inference of a language, since no practice of utterance that failed to abide by the law would be a language. If an utterance has a meaning there must, in general, be occasions on which it is correct and occasions on which it is incorrect to make it. This selective feature of its utterance constitutes the existence of a rule for its use. To impart such rules to others we must be able to correct their errors and for our own use to be critical we must be able to cancel our own mistakes. Language requires rule-governed utterance, and the existence of conventions of affirmation and negation is an indispensable minimum of rules. The difference between a language and a practice of making arbitrary noises is that the former embodies a concept of negation. And the law of contradiction is an essential part of all definitions of negation, even if the law of excluded middle is not. But this primacy does not show the law of contradiction to be non-conventional. To choose to speak rather than babble is, amongst other things, to accept the law of contradiction. But to speak is still a choice and the law of contradiction still a convention even though its abandonment would put us in a position where we should no longer be able to say, or even see, what we had done.

Most arguments against the view that necessity is conventional start by misstating it. Broad said that if necessary truths report the existence of linguistic conventions they must be synthetic and empirical. No doubt they would be but what the thesis says is that they are made necessary by convention not that they describe the conventions that prevail. To move your knight in accordance with the relevant rule of chess is not to say that that rule obtains. It is argued again that if to assert a necessary truth is to adopt a convention it would be a matter of free choice. But, according to the thesis, although the necessity of a statement *reflects* the existence of a convention its assertion is not ordinarily a way of *instituting* it. When you move your knight in accordance with the rules of chess you are not reinventing the game and when you move it in a currently forbidden way you are not setting up a new game of your own. Once in a while new conventions are set up in this comparatively inarticulate way. There is the case of William Webb Ellis who first picked up the ball and ran with it, thus inventing rugby football. The performance of a counter-conventional act may be striking enough to recommend a new convention by a concrete display of its possibilities. Poets are the chief William Webb Ellises of language.

A more serious objection, raised by Lewis in his *Analysis of Knowledge and Valuation*, is that the conventionality principle fails to distinguish sentences from the propositions they express. Since the meaning of a sentence is due to convention the fact that a sentence expresses a necessary proposition is conventional. But it does not follow, and is not the case, that the necessity of the proposition expressed is conventional. The relation of meanings in which it consists is an objective and timeless necessity which obtains whether anybody is aware of it, or has conventionally instituted any terms to express it, or not.

Some of the force of this argument is removed by the consideration that if it applies to any necessary truth it applies to all of them. Defenders of the synthetic *a priori* have usually wanted to distinguish between trifling, verbal, analytic necessities, such as 'all bald men are bald', and serious, substantial, synthetic ones, such as 'nothing can be red and green all over' or 'there is no largest prime number'. But if 'nothing can be red and green all over' owes its necessity to a non-conventional relation of meanings which it is used by convention to express then so does 'all bald men are bald'. If the convention governing the use of 'all' were exchanged for that now governing 'not all' the sentence 'all bald men are bald' would come to express a contradiction but the proposition it originally expressed would remain necessarily true. Supporters of the argument must then agree that no necessary propositions whatever are true by convention but that all sentences expressing necessary propositions are.

But even if Lewis's argument fails to distinguish two kinds of necessity it is still an objection to the thesis. I shall argue that the distinction it draws between the conventionally introduced relations between words in virtue of the meanings they have been given and the supposedly non-conventional relations between the meanings themselves cannot be drawn.

It will be simplest to consider it in application to verbal definitions, as a way of showing that they are not conventional. Both sides agree that the identity of meaning of two synonymous expressions is established by convention. But the anti-conventionalist maintains that there is a non-conventional identity of concepts, lying behind the conventional synonymy of terms, which would still exist even if no means of expressing the concepts had ever been devised. The actual use of the expressions 'bachelor' and 'unmarried man' is something that has been conventionally set up in the course of human history. But it is only because there is a non-conventional identity between the timeless and objective concepts that these terms have been chosen to express that the terms are synonymous.

There is a suggestive incoherence in the formulation of this principle about conceptual identity. On the one hand it says that there are two concepts involved, one corresponding to each of the synonymous expressions; on the other that there is only a single concept which is the meaning common to both. What has happened is that the anti-conventionalist has seen two senses in statements of identity of meaning where in fact there is only one. He wants to say that it is a matter of convention that the meaning of '*bachelor*' is the same as the meaning of '*unmarried man*' but that it is an objective fact that *this* concept (the one conventionally expressed by the word 'bachelor' as it happens) is identical with *this* one (the one conventionally expressed by the phrase 'unmarried man' as it happens). But identity-statements do not correlate objects considered in themselves, they can correlate objects only under a certain description. The only way in which concepts can be identifyingly described is by reference to the words that express them. Of course every concept, like everything else, is what it is. But we can only say what it is by correlating one description of it with another.

What suggests that there is an objective relation of self-identity, over and above the identity asserted of the concept under two descriptions, is the fact that I can know what the meaning of '*X*' is and know what the meaning of '*Y*' is without realizing that '*X*' and '*Y*' have the same meaning. But this is because I can know what the meaning of '*X*' is without knowing everything about the meaning of '*X*'. To know the meaning of a non-logical term, at any rate, is to be able to decide about any particular thing, actual or possible, whether or not the term applies to it. To decide whether two terms are the same in meaning I have to exercise this capacity by considering whether there is any particular thing, actual or possible, to which I would apply one term but not the other. The meaning is not some kind of wholly transparent object present to consciousness in all its details. Consider the identification of ordinary concrete objects. I can know which hook my coat is hanging on, the unpainted one let us say, and which hook your coat is hanging on, let us say the one nearest the light switch. But I may not realize that our coats are hanging on the same hook. I can be in a position to identify our respective hooks without realizing that they are one and the same. What I fail to realize is not the self-identity of an object considered in itself but that two descriptions, 'the unpainted hook' and 'the hook nearest the light switch' refer to the same thing.

The object referred to in a true identity-statement does not have, in itself, the duality which makes identification possible. Duality only comes in with the ways in which the object is described and conceived. One identity-statement can be grounded in another as the example about the hooks shows. But such a process of support will only replace some descriptions by others. It will never terminate in a statement in which the object, innocent of all description, will be identified with itself.

V

The third and final principle I have undertaken to derive from the thesis that necessary truth depends on meaning corresponds to Frege's definition of an analytic statement as one for whose proof nothing is required beyond logical laws and definitions of extra-logical terms. To accept the definition is not to endorse the view that all necessity is logical: Frege himself thought geometry was necessary but, in this sense, synthetic.

The outlines of an argument to prove that if necessity depends on meaning it depends on logic and definitions are to be found in Wittgenstein's *Tractatus*. How are the expressions given the meanings from which the necessity of statements arises? Either indirectly, by definition in terms of other expressions already understood, or in a direct way. The direct definition of non-logical terms is carried out by ostension, their correlation with observable features of the world. Logical terms are implicitly defined by means of logical laws. These logical laws, implicitly definitive of the basic logical terms, provide an initial stock of necessary truths. Others are generated by sub-stitution in them in accordance with explicit definitions. Two non-logical terms with the same ostensive definition can be explicitly defined in terms of each other. Two such terms with different ostensive definitions are distinct in meaning and thus not related in the way that gives rise to necessity. Therefore the only conventions of meaning that can render statements containing the terms they relate to necessary are (i) logical laws implicitly defining logical terms, (ii) explicit definitions and (iii) identical ostensive definitions of non-logical terms which could be replaced by explicit definitions of either in terms of the other.

An objection of principle to this argument is that it assumes that the expressions of our language can be exclusively separated into the logical and the non-logical. Though this may look a reasonable assumption at first glance in fact the argument does not represent logical and non-logical terms in a necessarily exclusive way. For it takes a logical term to be one whose meaning is *wholly* determined, in the end and after explicit definitions have been applied, by logical laws and a non-logical term to be one whose meaning is *wholly* determined, in the end, by ostension. It leaves out the possibility of mixed terms whose meaning is partly fixed by ostension and partly by the kind of implicit definition given for the basic logical terms. Simple descriptive predicates like 'red' suggest that this possibility is realized. It is not sufficient for an understanding of 'red' to have been shown enough red things to be able to tell whether further things are red or not. The use of the term must also be circumscribed by the realization that if a thing is red it cannot also be of another colour as well. Must we then admit that some necessities depend on non-logical laws, implicitly definitive of non-logical terms, as well as logical laws and explicit definitions? To decide this question we need a criterion for distinguishing between logical and non-logical laws and terms.

Before considering this obscurity in the principle that all necessity is logical and in the Fregean definition of 'analytic' to which it corresponds three preliminary points should be mentioned. First, Frege's definition draws some of its attraction from the idea that it improves on the Leibnizian definition in terms of identity and contradiction in that it does not accord a mistakenly elevated place to the traditional laws of thought. Russell and others thought this elevation to be a mistake because the ancient laws did not figure in any of the recognized sets of axioms sufficiently powerful for the derivation of ordinary logic. It may be that this dethronement was premature. We have already seen one reason for giving a special place to the law of contradiction; no system without it is a logic. Further-more it plays a fundamental part in two non-axiomatic methods of demonstration. It is the final court of appeal in demonstration by reductio ad absurdum (cf. K. R. Popper, 'Logic Without Assump-tions', *P. A. S.* 1946–7) and it is presupposed by the mechanical method of truth-tables in the rule that a sentence-element cannot have more than one truth-value (cf. G. H. von Wright, *Logical Studies*,

p. 8). Secondly, the contracted version of Frege's definition now in general currency as one true in virtue of logical laws alone or as one reducible with the help of definitions to a truth of logic has led some philosophers to conclude that the laws of logic are not themselves analytic (cf. W. T. Stace, *Theory of Knowledge and Existence*, p. 361; W. H. Walsh, *Reason and Experience*, p. 50). This is, of course, a misunderstanding. What is reducible to a law of logic is identical in meaning to it and must have the same logical status as it has. But it does point to a weakness of the Fregean definition which is that it wholly trivializes the statement that logical truths are analytic. It would certainly be an achievement to show that all necessity was logical but, in the first place, this does not throw any light on the nature of logical truths themselves and, secondly, it can only be done after it has first been shown that all necessary truths are analytic in the wider sense that they depend for their truth on their meaning.

The most serious deficiency of the Fregean definition, which must infect the corresponding principle, remains to be discussed: the fact that the concept of a logical law or truth on which it turns is thoroughly indeterminate. At one end the concept is firmly fixed by highly abstract elementary principles which would be universally accepted as laws of logic. But how far down into the body of truths as a whole does the class of logical truths extend?

One familiar and reasonable criterion for a statement's being a logical truth is that logical terms alone should occur essentially in it. When Russell made this suggestion, he was conscious of its limitations: it provides a necessary, but not a sufficient, condition of being a logical truth (*Introduction to Mathematical Philosophy*, p. 202). In the plainly contingent statements that something exists $((\exists x)x = x)$, that at least two things exist $((\exists x)(\exists y)x \neq y) \ldots$ logical terms alone occur essentially. The further necessary condition required to exclude such cases is that logical truths are necessary. If logical truth is thus defined as a necessary truth in which only logical terms occur essentially the principle corresponding to Frege's sense of 'analytic' takes the form: every necessary truth in which non-logical terms occur essentially can be reduced with the help of definitions to one in which they do not.

The crucial need at this point is for an account of logical terms to be given which is precise enough for the principle to be discussed. It would, of course, be circular to define a logical term as one that occurs essentially in a logical truth. Essential occurrence in necessary truths is not much better. In the first place it would make any term logical since every term occurs essentially in some necessary truth: 'bachelor' in 'all bachelors are unmarried', 'red' in 'nothing can be red and green all over'. Secondly, this proposal would trivialize the principle under discussion in equating logical and necessary truth by fiat.

Logicians in recent times, following Tarski, have been sceptical about arriving at any general criterion for logical terms. Quine simply enumerates a set of logical primitives, regarding these and anything wholly definable in terms of them as logical. He adheres to a roughly conformist principle of selection in assembling his primitives: it is the smallest set capable of yielding the vocabulary of what has traditionally passed as logic.

Can anything be done that it is less passive and more explanatory? It is an agreed and obvious feature of admitted logical terms that they are neutral as between topics and capable of figuring in discourse about any sort of subject-matter. I suggest that the essential character of logical terms can be made clearer if we reflect on the reasons for this fact. For it is a consequence of the particular way in which logical terms are endowed with meaning. Whereas topical, non-logical, terms are introduced, directly or indirectly, by some kind of ostension, which correlates them with particular regions or features of the extra-linguistic world, the topic-neutral terms of logic are introduced by implicit definition. For example, the ordinary concept of negation is introduced by the laws of contradiction and excluded middle, which are general formulae whose variable elements can take statements about any subject-matter whatever as their values. Logical terms are purely syntactical. Their function is to arrange or organize discourse, not to refer to anything in the extra-linguistic world. We can thus define a logical term as one whose meaning is wholly specified by implicit definitions.

In his justly celebrated essay *Truth By Convention* Quine makes an objection to this proposal, which has been very influential and is, I believe, mistaken. Comparing various ways in which mathematics might be reduced to logic he comes finally to the view that they might be identified as containing only terms whose meaning is wholly introducible by conventional assignment of truth to implicit definitions. His objection is that this criterion is wholly undiscriminating. Certainly sense can be given to 'not', 'if' and 'every' by implicit definition but so can it to every other term. The example he considers in detail is 'later than'. Its meaning can be fixed, he claims, by the conventional assignment of truth to all statements in which only 'later than' and the admitted logical primitives occur essentially. From this he infers that the technique can be extended to any term whatever.

Now the statements in which only 'later than' and the logical primitives occur essentially can indeed be regarded as logical truths. But they do not suffice to fix the sense of 'later than' and a part of this term, the element 'late', does not occur in them essentially. The relevant statements are that if x is later than y, is not later than x and that if x is later than y and y than z then x is later than z. These two statements are instances of general principles of asymmetry and transitivity for the radically topic-neutral term 'more than' or 'more ϕ than': $(x)\,(y)\,(\phi)\,(x > \phi y) \to\; \sim (y > \phi x)$ and $(x)\,(y)\,(z)\,(\phi)\,((x > \phi y).$ $(y > \phi z)) \to (x > \phi z)$. These wholly topic-neutral necessary truths give only part of the meaning of 'later than'. It must also be correlated with particular pairs of temporally distinct events. Statements reporting these indispensable correlative facts will not serve as implicit definitions. First, though this is not a reason that would weigh with Quine, because they are contingent. Secondly, because they must contain terms other than 'later than' and the logical primitives which occur essentially in them. These terms will identify the temporally distinct events involved, as in 'the accession of Richard I is later than the accession of Henry I'.

The account I have given of logical terms contains the defensible part of the theory of innate ideas. Logical concepts are not acquired by ostension. The attempts of Russell and others to find empirical correlates for the logical terms in the feelings of their users have been much criticized. Geach has pointed out (*Mental Acts*, p. 23) that a feeling of hesitation does not universally accompany the use of 'or', a threatening feeling is quite as appropriate. Also it is hard to see what feeling is to go with 'and', 'if' and 'all'. But the crucial point is that the feelings that accompany a logical term are not criteria for their correct use. An extreme of hesitation on my part does not make a statement of the form 'p or q' true. Logical concepts are innate in the harmless sense of being not empirical but syntactical.

The necessary transitivity of 'later than' is not, then a refutation of the principle that all necessity is logical. It is an instance of a logical truth in which only 'and', 'if', the universal quantifier and the topic-neutral term 'more ϕ than' occur essentially, while the element 'late', with its topical reference to time, occurs vacuously. There is, however, a difficulty here which was pointed out to me by Mr. P. F. Strawson. The principles of asymmetry and transitivity do not wholly fix the sense of 'more ϕ than' since they remain necessarily true if 'less ϕ than' is substituted and 'more' and 'less' do not mean the same. But however this objection is to be dealt with it does not show 'more ϕ than' to be a non-logical term. For the difference between 'more' and 'less' must be as topic-neutral as they are.

Can we deal with 'nothing can be red and green all over', which is equally resistant to reduction to ordinary logical laws, in the same way? The only definition of 'red' that would make 'this is red and green' reducible to an explicit contradiction defines 'red' as 'not green and not blue and . . . ' It is objectionable, first, because it is open-ended and, secondly, because it can only be applied to one colour term if circularity is to be avoided and in that case 'nothing can be blue and white all over' and the rest still resist reduction.

It could be said that 'nothing can be red and green all over' is an instance of the highly abstract law: 'nothing can be a member of two species of a genus'. Like the transitivity of 'more ϕ than' it fixes only part of the sense of the terms involved but it is as topic-neutral as could be wished. This is too informal a step to settle the question of whether all necessity is logical. But it does formulate the question in a way that allows it to be settled by decision. If the principle is interpreted narrowly, as saying that all necessary truths can be reduced with the help of definitions to necessary truths in which only terms whose meaning is *wholly* given by implicit definitions occur essentially, then 'nothing can be red and green all over' is a falsifying exception to it. If, on the other hand, it is interpreted broadly, as saying that all necessary truths implicitly define their terms or are reducible to those that do, the principle is correct.

VI

So far I have taken it for granted that there is a distinction between the necessary and the contingent, and my aim has been to show that it coincides with four other distinctions all of which have been taken to distinguish the analytic from the synthetic: (i) statements true in virtue of meaning and of experience, (ii) statements which assert no more and more than they assume, (iii) statements true by convention and on non-conventional grounds and (iv) statements logically and non-logically true. Quine's critique of analyticity questions the assumption I have made that there is a distinction to discuss. Against the logical dualism which sees a fundamental difference of kind between necessary and contingent he sees only continuity.

There is an interesting peculiarity about the tactics of his argument.

The concept of synonymy whose intelligibility he questions is not really central to the Fregean definition of 'analytic statement' as either a truth of logic or else reducible to one by the replacement of synonyms by synonyms on which he concentrates. Even if his objections to synonymy were well-founded his argument would not show that there are no analytic statements. It would show, rather, that explicit truths of logic were the only unequivocally analytic statements. His argument has more damaging implications but they are rhetorically suggested rather than argued for. If all and only logical truths are analytic the term 'analytic' explains nothing about logical truth and is not worth introducing. Furthermore his defeatist account of logical truth in terms of a pretty arbitrarily enumerated set of logical primitives, the consequence of his mistaken belief that any term whatever can have its whole sense given by implicit definition, implies that there is no important difference of kind between logical and non-logical truths. Finally if there is no clear concept of synonymy the Leibnizian principle which grounds necessity on the fact that what some statements assert is partly or wholly identical in meaning with what they assume falls to the ground. But the direct force of his argument is restricted by the limitations of the Fregean concept of the analytic on which it turns.

But how well-founded are his doubts about synonymy? Grice and Strawson have shown that the supposed circle of intensional terms—synonymous, analytic, contradictory, etc.—which cannot be defined except in terms of one another can be broken (*Philosophical Review*, 1956). 'Synonymous' means the same as 'means the same as' and the latter is no philosopher's technicality but a perfectly familiar expression. An idea does not become technical simply by being dressed up in an ungainly polysyllable. I shall develop this argument by showing that Quine cannot consistently raise the doubt he does about the concept of synonymy unless he already understands it.

How, he asks, are relations of synonymy to be discovered? By the observation of linguistic behaviour. He confines this observation to the application of terms by those who understand them. But all that application can show is identity of extension which according to defenders of analyticity is not the same as, even if it follows from, identity of meaning. Synonymy, he infers, is empirically undiscoverable.

But why should observation of linguistic behaviour be only of the application of terms and not of the learning that preceded it? We learn to use words both ostensively, by noticing and imitating the applications made by the fully-fledged language-users around us, and lexically, by becoming aware of the conventionally established identity of meaning between new words and words whose meaning we already understand. These processes are more closely interwoven, no doubt, than the theory of simple and complex ideas allows but there are pure cases: 'horses' ostensive and 'bachelor' lexical.

Now Quine deprives himself, as linguistic observer, of reliance on the fact of lexical learning which was part of his training as a linguistic agent. This cannot be reasonable unless language is wholly ostensive and there is no such thing as lexical learning. If that were the case there would be no word-word correlations to observe but only word-thing correlations. We should have to learn the use of 'featherless biped' as we now learn the use of 'man'. But in that case the two terms would have the same meaning. In a purely ostensive language there would be no difference between coextensiveness and synonymy. If exactly the same ostensible specimens will serve equally well for the introduction of either term each will be associated with the same recognitional capacity. It would be idle to envisage deviant applications of the two terms. It would be a conjecture, with no more evidence in its favour than that there are the two different terms, about the possibility of deviating application in the future by more expert language-users than oneself.

We can envisage a featherless biped that is not a man because 'featherless biped' is a lexically learnt term. It is learnt through the rather undramatic lexical formula: 'x is a featherless biped' = 'x is featherless and x is a biped'. Idioms like 'French polisher' show that this formula cannot be generalized without qualification: not all French polishers are French. The two elements in the defining part of the formula are learnt ostensively and the extension of the defined term is fixed indirectly as the logical product of the extensions of its constituents. There are plenty of non-men in these constituent extensions: snakes and chickens, for example. Terms can only be co-extensive without identity of meaning if there are antecedent relations of synonymy that fix indirectly the extensions of at least one of the terms involved. In Quine's ostensive language, all true biconditionals like 'all and only men are featherless bipeds' would be analytic. Observation of linguistic behaviour restricted to application alone could only discover coextensiveness that did not entail identity of meaning in a language that contained lexically learnt terms and thus allowed for a less restricted kind of observation. In both types of language 'this is a featherless biped' would be synthetic and so the analytic-synthetic distinction would persist in a purely ostensive language. The synthetic biconditionals which, according to Quine, are all that linguistic observation can discover, could only exist in a language where the conventional assertion of analytic biconditionals was part of the learning process.

It is not *inconceivable* that ostensively learnt terms with the same extension should differ in meaning. Mr. D. F. Pears has pointed out to me that a learner might connect two such coextensive terms with different recurrent aspects or features of the common stock of situations with which they were correlated. But this would be gratuitous in the circumstances. Ostension correlates a term with a class of spatio-temporal regions. Though several distinct common properties or resemblances may characterize such a class it will be natural for learners to fasten on the most obvious of them (cf. my 'Properties and Classes', *P.A.S.*, 1958–9). What makes such differing interpretations seem likely is that we can conceive, for example, that all and only things of a certain shape, say sea-shells, might be of a certain colour, say pink. We should retain distinct concepts of seashell and pink provided there was no general coincidence of particular shapes with particular colours. In the absence of such a coincidence we could form the generic concepts of shape and colour and use them to guide or focus the learning of 'sea-shell' and 'pink' ('this *thing* is a seashell', 'this is pink in *colour*'). But then they would not be purely ostensive terms.

VIII

THE MEANING OF LOGICAL CONNECTIVES

(1) THE RUNABOUT INFERENCE-TICKET

A. N. PRIOR

IT is sometimes alleged that there are inferences whose validity arises solely from the meanings of certain expressions occurring in them. The precise technicalities employed are not important, but let us say that such inferences, if any such there be, are analytically valid.

One sort of inference which is sometimes said to be in this sense analytically valid is the passage from a conjunction to either of its conjuncts, e.g., the inference 'Grass is green and the sky is blue, therefore grass is green'. The validity of this inference is said to arise solely from the meaning of the word 'and'. For if we are asked what is the meaning of the word 'and', at least in the purely conjunctive sense (as opposed to, e.g., its colloquial use to mean 'and then'), the answer is said to be *completely* given by saying that (i) from any pair of statements P and Q we can infer the statement formed by joining P to Q by 'and' (which statement we hereafter describe as 'the statement P-and-Q'), that (ii) from any conjunctive statement P-and-Q we can infer P, and (iii) from P-and-Q we can always infer Q. Anyone who has learnt to perform these inferences knows the meaning of 'and', for there is simply nothing more *to* knowing the meaning of 'and' than being able to perform these inferences.

A doubt might be raised as to whether it is really the case that, for any pair of statements P and Q, there is always a statement R such that given P and given Q we can infer R, and given R we can infer P and can also infer Q. But on the view we are considering such a doubt is quite misplaced, once we have introduced a word, say the word 'and', precisely in order to form a statement R with these properties from any pair of statements P and Q. The doubt reflects the old superstitious view that an expression must have some independently determined meaning before we can discover whether

From *Analysis*, Vol. 21 (Blackwell, 1960), pp. 38–39. Reprinted by permission of the author, *Analysis*, and Basil Blackwell.

inferences involving it are valid or invalid. With analytically valid inferences this just isn't so.

I hope the conception of an analytically valid inference is now at least as clear to my readers as it is to myself. If not, further illumination is obtainable from Professor Popper's paper on 'Logic without Assumptions' in *Proceedings of the Aristotelian Society* for 1946–7, and from Professor Kneale's contribution to *Contemporary British Philosophy*, Volume III. I have also been much helped in my understanding of the notion by some lectures of Mr. Strawson's and some notes of Mr. Hare's.

I want now to draw attention to a point not generally noticed, namely that in this sense of 'analytically valid' any statement whatever may be inferred, in an analytically valid way, from any other. '2 and 2 are 5', for instance, from '2 and 2 are 4'. It is done in two steps, thus:

2 and 2 are 4.
Therefore, 2 and 2 are 4 tonk 2 and 2 are 5.
Therefore, 2 and 2 are 5.

There may well be readers who have not previously encountered this conjunction 'tonk', it being a comparatively recent addition to the language; but it is the simplest matter in the world to explain what it means. Its meaning is completely given by the rules that (i) from any statement P we can infer any statement formed by joining P to any statement Q by 'tonk' (which compound statement we hereafter describe as 'the statement P-tonk-Q'), and that (ii) from any 'contonktive' statement P-tonk-Q we can infer the contained statement Q.

A doubt might be raised as to whether it is really the case that, for any pair of statements P and Q, there is always a statement R such that given P we can infer R, and given R we can infer Q. But this doubt is of course quite misplaced, now that we have introduced the word 'tonk' precisely in order to form a statement R with these properties from any pair of statements P and Q.

As a matter of simple history, there have been logicians of some eminence who have seriously doubted whether sentences of the form 'P and Q' express single propositions (and so, e.g., have negations). Aristotle himself, in *De Soph. Elench.* 176 a 1 ff., denies that 'Are Callias and Themistocles musical?' is a single question; and J. S. Mill says of 'Caesar is dead and Brutus is alive' that 'we might as well call a street a complex house, as these two propositions a complex proposition' (*System of Logic* I, iv. 3). So it is not to be wondered at if the form 'P tonk Q' is greeted at first with similar scepticism. But more enlightened views will surely prevail at last, especially when men consider the extreme *convenience* of the new form, which promises to banish *falsche Spitfizndigkeit* from Logic for ever.

(2)   TONK, PLONK AND PLINK[1]

Nuel D. Belnap

A. N. Prior has recently discussed[2] the connective *tonk*, where *tonk* is defined by specifying the role it plays in inference. Prior characterizes the role of *tonk* in inference by describing how it behaves as conclusion, and as premise: (1) $A \vdash A\text{-}tonk\text{-}B$, (2) $A\text{-}tonk\text{-}B \vdash B$ (where we have used the sign '$\vdash$' for deducibility). We are then led by the transitivity of deducibility to the validity of $A \vdash B$, "which promises to banish *falsche Spitzfindigkeit* from Logic for ever".

A possible moral to be drawn is that connectives cannot be defined in terms of deducibility at all; that, for instance, it is illegitimate to define *and* as that connective such that (1) $A\text{-}and\text{-}B \vdash A$, (2) $A\text{-}and\text{-}B \vdash B$, and (3) $A, B \vdash A\text{-}and\text{-}B$. We must first, so the moral goes, have a notion of what *and* means, independently of the role it plays as premise and as conclusion. Truth-tables are one way of specifying this antecedent meaning; this seems to be the moral drawn by J. T. Stevenson.[3] There are good reasons, however, for defending the legitimacy of defining connectives in terms of the roles they play in deductions.

It seems plain that throughout the whole texture of philosophy one can distinguish two modes of explanation: the analytic mode, which tends to explain wholes in terms of parts, and the synthetic mode, which explains parts in terms of the wholes or contexts in which they occur.[4] In logic, the analytic mode would be represented by Aristotle, who commences with terms as the ultimate atoms, explains propositions or judgements by means of these, syllogisms by means of the propositions which go to make them up, and finally ends with the

From *Analysis*, Vol. 22 (Blackwell, 1962), pp. 130–4. Reprinted by permission of the author, *Analysis*, and Basil Blackwell.

[1]This research was supported in part by the Office of Naval Research, Group Psychology Branch, Contract No. SAR/Nonr-609(16).

[2]'The Runabout Inference-Ticket', *Analysis* 21.2, (Dec. 1960).

[3]'Roundabout the Runabout Inference-Ticket', *Analysis* 21.6, (June 1961). Cf. p. 127: 'The important difference between the theory of analytic validity [Prior's phrase for what is here called the synthetic view] as it should be stated and as Prior stated it lies in the fact that he gives the meaning of connectives in terms of permissive rules, whereas they should be stated in terms of truth-function statements in a meta-language'.

[4]I learned this way of looking at the matter from R. S. Brumbaugh.

notion of a science as a tissue of syllogisms. The analytic mode is also represented by the contemporary logician who first explains the meaning of complex sentences, by means of truth-tables, as a function of their parts, and then proceeds to give an account of correct inference in terms of the sentences occurring therein. The *locus classicus* of the application of the synthetic mode is, I suppose, Plato's treatment of justice in the *Republic*, where he defines the just man by reference to the larger context of the community. Among formal logicians, use of the synthetic mode in logic is illustrated by Kneale and Popper (cited by Prior), as well as by Jaskowski, Gentzen, Fitch, and Curry, all of these treating the meaning of connectives as arising from the role they play in the context of formal inference. It is equally well illustrated, I think, by aspects of Wittgenstein and those who learned from him to treat the meanings of words as arising from the role they play in the context of discourse. It seems to me nearly self-evident that employment of both modes of explanation is important and useful. It would therefore be truly a shame to see the synthetic mode in logic pass away as a result of a severe attack of tonktitis.

Suppose, then, that we wish to hold that it is after all possible to define connectives contextually, in terms of deducibility. How are we to prevent tonktitis? How are we to make good the claim that there is no connective such as *tonk*[1] though there is a connective such as *and* (where *tonk* and *and* are defined as above)?

It seems to me that the key to a solution[2] lies in observing that even on the synthetic view, we are not defining our connectives *ab initio*, but rather in terms of an *antecedently given context of deducibility*, concerning which we have some definite notions. By that I mean that before arriving at the problem of characterizing connectives, we have already made some assumptions about the nature of deducibility. That this is so can be seen immediately by observing Prior's use of the transitivity of deducibility in order to secure his ingenious result.

---

[1] That there is no meaningful proposition expressed by A-*tonk*-B; that there is no meaningful sentence A-*tonk*-B—distinctions suggested by these alternative modes of expression are irrelevant. Not myself being a victim of eidophobia, I will continue to use language which treats the connective-word '*tonk*' as standing for the putative propositional connective, *tonk*. It is equally irrelevant whether we take the sign ⊢ as representing a syntactic concept of deducibility or a semantic concept of deducibility or a semantic concept of logical consequence.

[2] Prior's note is a gem, reminding one of Lewis Carroll's 'What the Tortoise said to Achilles'. And as for the latter, so for the former, I suspect that no solution will ever be universally accepted as *the* solution.

But if we note that we already *have* some assumptions about the context of deducibility within which we are operating, it becomes apparent that by a too careless use of definitions, it is possible to create a situation in which we are forced to say things inconsistent with those assumptions.

The situation is thus exactly analogous to that, pointed out by Peano, which occurs when one attempts to define an operation, '?', on rational numbers as follows:

$$\left(\frac{a}{b} ? \frac{c}{d}\right) \ = \ _{df} \ \frac{a+c}{b+d}.$$

This definition is inadmissible precisely because it has consequences which contradict prior assumptions; for, as can easily be shown, admitting this definition would lead to (say) $\frac{2}{3} = \frac{3}{5}$.

In short, we can distinguish between the admissibility of the definition of *and* and the inadmissibility of *tonk* on the grounds of consistency—i.e., consistency with antecedent assumptions. We can give a precise account of the requirement of consistency from the synthetic point of view as follows.

(1) We consider some characterization of deducibility, which may be treated as a formal system, i.e., as a set of axioms and rules involving the sign of deducibility, '$\vdash$', where '$A_1, \ldots, A_n \vdash B$' is read 'B is deducible from $A_1, \ldots, A_n$.' For definiteness, we shall choose as our characterization the structural rules of Gentzen:

Axiom.	$A \vdash A$	
Rules.	*Weakening:*	from $A_1, \ldots, A_n \vdash C$ to infer $A_1, \ldots, A_n \, B \vdash C$
	Permutation:	from $A_1, \ldots, A_i, A_{i+1}, \ldots, A_n \vdash B$ to infer $A_1, \ldots, A_{i+1}, A_i, \ldots, A_n \vdash B$.
	Contraction:	from $A_1, \ldots, A_n, A_n \vdash B$ to infer $A_1, \ldots, A_n \vdash B$
	Transitivity:	from $A_1, \ldots, A_m \vdash B$ and $C_1, \ldots, C_n, B \vdash D$ to infer $A_1, \ldots, A_m, C_1, \ldots, C_n \vdash D$.

In accordance with the opinions of experts (or even perhaps on more substantial grounds) we may take this little system as expressing all and only the universally valid statements and rules expressible in the given notation: it completely determines the context.

(2) We may consider the proposed definition of some connective, say *plonk*, as an *extension* of the formal system characterizing deducibility, and an extension in two senses. (a) The notion of sentence

is extended by introducing A-*plonk*-B as a sentence, whenever A and B are sentences. (b) We add some axioms or rules governing A-*plonk*-B as occurring as one of the premisses or as conclusion of a deducibility-statement. These axioms or rules constitute our definition of *plonk* in terms of the role it plays in inference.

(3) We may now state the demand for the consistency of the definition of the new connective, *plonk*, as follows: the extension must be *conservative*[1]; i.e., although the extension may well have new deducibility-statements, these new statements will all involve *plonk*. The extension will not have any new deducibility-statements which do not involve *plonk* itself. It will not lead to any deducibility-statement $A_1, \ldots, A_n \vdash B$ not containing *plonk*, unless that statement is already provable in the absence of the *plonk*-axioms and *plonk*-rules. The justification for unpacking the demand for consistency in terms of conservativeness is precisely our antecedent assumption that we already had *all* the universally valid deducibility-statements not involving any special connectives.

So the trouble with the definition of *tonk* given by Prior is that it is inconsistent. It gives us an extension of our original character-ization of deducibility which is not conservative, since in the extension (but not in the original) we have, for arbitrary A and B, $A \vdash B$. Adding a tonkish role to the deducibility-context would be like adding to cricket a player whose role was so specified as to make it impossible to distinguish winning from losing.

Hence, given that our characterization of deducibility is taken as complete, we may with propriety say 'There is no such connective as *tonk*'; just as we say that there is no operation, '?', on rational numbers such that $\left(\dfrac{a}{b} \, ? \, \dfrac{c}{d} \right) = \dfrac{a + c}{b + d}$. On the other hand, it is easily shown that the extension got by adding *and* is conservative, and we may hence say 'There *is* a connective having these properties'.

It is good to keep in mind that the question of the existence of a connective having such and such properties is relative to our charac-terization of deducibility. If we had initially allowed $A \vdash B$ (!), there would have been no objection to *tonk*, since the extension would then have been conservative. Also, there would have been no inconsistency had we omitted from our characterization of deducibility the rule of transitivity.

The mathematical analogy leads us to ask if we ought not also to

---

[1] The notion of conservative extensions is due to Emil Post.

add *uniqueness*[1] as a requirement for connectives introduced by definitions in terms of deducibility (although clearly this requirement is not as essential as the first, or at least not in the same way). Suppose, for example, that I propose to define a connective *plonk* by specifying that B ⊢ A-*plonk*-B. The extension is easily shown to be conservative, and we may, therefore, say 'There is a connective having these properties'. But is there only one? It seems rather odd to say we have defined *plonk* unless we can show that A-*plonk*-B is a function of A and B, i.e., given A and B, there is only one proposition A-*plonk*-B. But what do we mean by uniqueness when operating from a synthetic, contextualist point of view? Clearly that at most *one* inferential role is permitted by the characterization of *plonk*; i.e., that there cannot be two connectives which share the characterization given to *plonk* but which otherwise sometimes play different roles. Formally put, uniqueness means that if exactly the same properties are ascribed to some other connective, say *plink*, then A-*plink*-B will play exactly the same role in inference as A-*plonk*-B, both as premiss and as conclusion. To say that *plonk* (characterized thus and so) describes a unique way of combining A and B is to say that if *plink* is given a characterization formally identical to that of *plonk*, then

(1) $A_1, ..., B$-*plonk*-$C, ..., A_n ⊢ D$ if and only if $A_1, ..., B$-*plink*-$C, ..., A_n ⊢ D$ and

(2) $A_1, ..., A_n ⊢ B$-*plonk*-C if and only if $A_1, ..., A_n ⊢ B$-*plink*-C.

Whether or not we can show this will depend, of course, not only on the properties ascribed to the connectives, but also on the properties ascribed to deducibility. Given the characterization of deducibility above, it is sufficient and necessary that B-*plonk*-C ⊢ B-*plink*-C, and conversely.

Harking back now to the definition of *plonk* by: B ⊢ A-*plonk*-B, it is easy to show that *plonk* is *not* unique; that given only: B ⊢ A-*plonk*-B, and B ⊢ A-*plink*-B, we cannot show that *plonk* and *plink* invariably play the same role in inference. Hence, the possibility arises that *plonk* and *plink* stand for different connectives: the conditions on *plonk* do not determine a unique connective. On the other hand, if we introduce a connective, *et*, with the same characterization as *and*, it will turn out that A-*and*-B and A-*et*-B play exactly the same role in inference. The conditions on *and* therefore do determine a unique connective.

Though it is difficult to draw a moral from Prior's delightful note

---

[1] Application to connectives of the notions of existence and uniqueness was suggested to me by a lecture of H. Hiz.

without being plonking, I suppose we might put it like this: one *can* define connectives in terms of deducibility, but one bears the onus of proving at least consistency (existence); and if one wishes further to talk about *the* connective (instead of *a* connective) satisfying certain conditions, it is necessary to prove uniqueness as well. But it is not necessary to have an antecedent idea of the independent meaning of the connective.

IX

TYPES AND ONTOLOGY

FRED SOMMERS

IN THIS paper[1] I shall be examining several notions of *types* which have important application in natural languages. I shall show that one of Russell's definitions of a type can be combined with one of Ryle's to give us two other and more powerful type conceptions which are free of the criticisms advanced against each of the former. The results cast considerable light on the relation of 'a language' to the sorts of things one can use the language to make statements about; for example, it becomes clear that the number of 'sorts of things' discriminated by any natural language is always finite. But far more important, the new type concepts enable us to exhibit formally the type structure of any natural language. It is this structure which determines the way the language discriminates different sorts of things. Since the question of ontology is 'What sorts of things are there?' the results may be construed as a formal ontology. The old Russell programme for an ontology which is defined by a logically correct (or corrected) language is thereby reinstated, though in a revised form. That programme has foundered on the type problem for natural languages. Black, for example, has brought out grave difficulties in Russell's type theory as it applies to natural languages, and he used those difficulties to promote scepticism about the Russell programme. But if I am right, a simple and adequate theory of types governs natural language and dictates its ontological commitments to different sorts of things.

From *Philosophical Review*, Vol. 72 (1963), pp. 327–63. Reprinted, with minor corrections, by permission of the author and the *Philosophical Review*.

[1] There are four sections to the paper. Section I isolates the problem of types for natural language and develops four type concepts appropriate to it. Section II reformulates these concepts syntactically and reconsiders Black's general criticism of a formal theory of types for natural language. In Section III the relation of types to ambiguity, and a problem raised by Black, is examined in detail. Section IV is constructive; the type-structural principle is stated and proved. The ontological meaning of the principle is discussed and the principle is illustratively applied.

I

The difference between the ordinary class notion and the notion of a 'sort' or a type is essential for an understanding of what ontologists are interested in. The ontologist says that the three classes of men, odd numbers, and even numbers are contained in two 'sorts' of things. It might be said that the ontologist has in mind a more general kind of class. (Thus Quine appears to think that the difference between the zoologist and the ontologist is only breadth of interest.)[1] But that leaves open the crucial question: what kind of generality interests the ontologist? Of course a 'sort' is a class, but what *kind* of class?

In asking that question we are asking for certain logical characteristics which distinguish types or sorts from other classes. Categories, types, sorts—all these terms have been used by philosophers—are classes of a special kind. We might call such a class an ontological class; but this would only add to the list of obscure synonyms even if it did serve to remind us that a clarification of the type question will help us to understand ontology as a branch of philosophy. In the early sections of this paper I shall use the word 'type'. The advantage of dealing with 'type' (over 'sort', 'category', 'ontological class', and so forth) lies in the fact that recent literature has given 'type' some precise technical meanings.

One clear answer to the question 'What is a type?' comes from Russell:

The definition of a logical type is as follows: *A* and *B* are of the same logical type if, and only if, given any fact of which *A* is a constituent, there is a corresponding fact which has *B* as a constituent, which either results by substituting *B* for *A* or is the negation of what so results. To take an illustration, Socrates and Aristotle are of the same type, because 'Socrates was a philosopher' and 'Aristotle was a philosopher' are both facts; Socrates and Caligula are of the same type, because 'Socrates was a philosopher' and 'Caligula was not a philosopher' are both facts. To love and to kill are of the same type, because 'Plato loved Socrates' and 'Plato did not kill Socrates' are both facts.[2]

Russell here defines a type as a class of things or relations. I shall ignore relations.

Confining ourselves to the criterion for type sameness as it applies to things, we have the following: Two things are of the same type with

[1] For an explicit statement of a view of ontology that does *not* logically distinguish it as a special discipline, see Quine's *Word and Object* (Cambridge, Mass., 1960), p. 275.

[2] *Contemporary British Philosophy* (London and New York, 1924), I, 371.

respect to a monadic predicate P, if and only if P is significantly (that is, truly or falsely but not absurdly) predicable of both. All the things of which it makes sense to predicate P belong to the same type. When P = 'is a philosopher', Julius Caesar and Socrates are of the same type with respect to p, but Julius Caesar and the Industrial Revolution are not of the same type with respect to P.

Since, as we shall see, Russell's type concept is only one of four fundamental type notions, it will be convenient to designate a set of things which meet Russell's specifications for a type by some special name. We shall call such a set an 'α-type'. Also, we shall say that every member of an α-type is 'spanned' by the predicate which defines it. (A predicate will be said to span a thing if it is predicated of it either truly or falsely but not absurdly.) Thus an α-type may be defined as a set of all and only those things that are spanned by some (monadic) predicate.

A second and different notion of types is to be found in Ryle's idea of a type or category mistake. Where Russell's formulation is material, Ryle's is formal or syntactical. A type or category mistake is made by any sentence which conjoins two expressions (predicates) that are not both significantly applicable to the same thing. Thus 'a sedan chair' and 'a flood of tears' cannot both be applied to the same thing. We cannot, for example, say that both expressions apply to what a young lady came home in: 'She came home in a sedan chair and a flood of tears' is therefore a type mistake. But this is true of any category mistake. 'Vanity' and 'feeling' are expressions which cannot both apply to some one thing together; the same is true of 'itch' and 'mood'. In calling 'Vanity is a feeling' and 'An itch is a mood' type mistakes, Ryle is evidently using 'type' for a class of *expressions*.

Confining ourselves once again to monadic predicates, we can arrive at a formulation. If P and Q are monadic predicates which can both be significantly applied to any one thing, then a sentence (P, Q) is not a type mistake; that is, P and Q are expressions of the same type. And in general, if t is some given thing, then the set of all and only all those predicates which span (are significantly predicable of) t form a type. We shall call this sort of predicate-set a 'B-type'.

Where Russell has defined a type to be a set of things spanned by a given predicate, Ryle's type-concept is that of a set of expressions which span some given thing. Russell's α-type and Ryle's B-type suffer from this relativity to some specific predicate or thing. And it is hardly surprising that Black's criticism of Russell can easily be generalized to apply to Ryle's conception of a *B*-type.

For Black in his criticism of Russell[1] showed that the notion of an α-type renders the relation of 'being of the same type' a non-transitive relation. Thus if a and b are things of the same α-type, while b and c are also of the same α-type, it does not follow that a and c are of the same α-type. For a and b may be of the same α-type with respect to P, while b and c may be of the same α-type with respect to Q. For example, let $a =$ Aristotle, $b =$ Bertrand Russell, $c =$ continuity, $P =$ (is) a philosopher and $Q =$ (is) thought about. Ryle's criterion for types of expressions suffers similarly from the nontransitivity of the relation 'being of the same *B*-type'. For suppose '(is) a philosopher' and '(is) thought about' are of the same *B*-type since both span Plato, while 'is thought about' and 'even prime' are of the same *B*-type since both span the second natural number. It does not follow that '(is) a philosopher' and '(is) an even prime' are of the same *B*-type. Here again it is the introduction of those 'high' predicates—like '(is) interesting', '(is) thought about'—which exposes the difficulty. We may therefore put Black's criticism in its general form: the existence of high predicates like 'is interesting', and so forth renders Russell's and Ryle's criteria for type sameness inadequate. *We require type notions that retain transitivity for the relation 'is of the same type'.*

Russell's α-types are sets of things; Ryle's *B*-types are sets of predicates. Corresponding to Russell's α-types we want now to define a type of thing for which 'being of the same type' is transitive without qualification. We shall call such a set of things a 'β-type'. Similarly, corresponding to Ryle's *B*-types we shall define a set of predicates—which we shall call an *A*-type—for which type sameness is transitive. More specifically, we use the concept of a *B*-type to define β-types while the notion of a α-type is used to define an *A*-type.

Consider some one thing t and the set of all those predicates such that any member of the set is predicable significantly of t. Such a predicate set we are calling a *B*-type. For example, let $t =$ Thales. Then in the *B*-type of t there will be predicate expressions like 'happy', 'married', 'bachelor', 'carpenter', 'weighs one hundred pounds', 'brown', and so forth. Outside the set there will be predicates like 'holiday', 'prime number', 'legal', and so forth. It is evident that the

[1] Max Black, 'Russell's Philosophy of Language', in *The Philosophy of Bertrand Russell* (ed. by P. A. Schilpp; Evanston and Chicago, 1944), p. 238.

same B-type will be unique for other individuals besides Thales. Thus using the B-type, we can define a set of things (a β-type) any one of which entertains predication by all and only all of the members of that B-type. More formally:

1. Two things are of the same β-type if the B-types for both are identical.
2. A β-type is a set of things all of whose members are spanned by predicates of some B-type and none of whose members is spanned by any predicate outside of that B-type.

It is obvious that for β-types, the relation 'being of the same type' is transitive. Also on the criterion for β-type sameness, it is clear that Russell and continuity are of different types, since while they share some spanning predicates (such as 'is thought about'), they do not share all. On the other hand, Socrates and Julius Caesar *are* of the same type since whatever spans one spans the other and nothing which spans one fails to span the other.

The three type concepts so far defined are:

1. α-types: a set of *things* constitutes an α-type with respect to a predicate P if and only if P spans all of the things in the set and nothing outside the set.
2. B-types: a set of *predicates* constitutes a B-type with respect to an individual t if and only if t is spanned by every member of the set and by no predicate outside the set.
3. β-types: a set of things constitutes a β-type if and only if every member of the set is spanned by every member of the same B-type and no member of the set is spanned by any predicate outside of that B-type.

Our fourth type concept is therefore:

4. A-types: a set of predicates constitutes an A-type if and only if every member of the set spans every member of some α-type and no member of the set spans a thing outside of that α-type.[1]

---

[1] For a formulation of a similar notion see A. Pap's last paper, 'Types and Meaninglessness', *Mind*, LXIX (1960), 48. See also my paper 'The Ordinary Language Tree', *Mind*, LXVIII (1959).

The notion of spanning is fundamental to all four type concepts; essentially they are defined in terms of it. It is evident that for any language of finite vocabulary—and every natural language is finite in that sense—the number of α-types spanned by the predicates is finite. The number of β-types is even smaller than the number of α-types and it too is finite. We may therefore conclude that the sorts of things (in either of the above senses of 'sorts') discriminated by any natural language is finite. Whether we define a sort or type of thing by what is spanned by a single predicate, or whether we define it by what is spanned by a set of predicates (and the combinatory possibilities for unique sets is limited for a finite vocabulary), we cannot have more than a finite number of sorts of things talked about by the same language.

Finally, by the above definitions the number of A-types corresponds exactly to the number of α-types, and the number of B-types corresponds exactly to the number of β-types, so that for all four senses of 'type' the number of types in any natural language is finite.

II

We have so far used the semantic concept of spanning to define B-types. But B-types can very usefully be defined in syntactical terms. Consider a set of expressions, $A', B', C' \ldots K'$, that can serve as grammatical predicates in subject predicate sentences. Thus A' might be 'is Socrates', B' might be 'is a philosopher', C' might be 'is an even prime', and so on. We shall speak of a corresponding set of $A, B, C \ldots K$ as a set of *terms*. Where $A' = $ 'is Socrates', $A = $ 'Socrates'; where B' 'is a philosopher', $B = $ 'philosopher'; and so on for the rest of the terms of the set.

Now let any pair of terms (X, Y) represent some sentence which conjoins the terms X and Y. Thus (X, Y) will be a sentence like 'X is Y', 'Some Y is X', 'All non-Y is X' and so on for all the logical forms of sentences conjoining the two terms X and Y. Let us suppose that $(X, Y)_i$ represents some one sentence with X and Y and that $(X, Y)_j$ represents some other sentence whose logical form differs from that of $(X, Y)_i$. We now state the syntactical equivalence. For any term X and Y and for any forms i and j:

(1) $\qquad (X, Y)_i$ is significant $\equiv (X, Y)_j$ is significant.

This equivalence expresses the simple fact that when a sentence (X, Y) is significant it remains significant under all the normal logical operations such as conversion, negation, contraposition, and so forth. And, similarly, if the sentence is category nonsense, then all such transformations are also nonsensical.

The significance or nonsignificance of a sentence $(X, Y)_i$ is therefore independent of the omnibus operator 'i'. Whether the sentence is significant depends only on what X and Y are. We may therefore ignore the logical form of the sentence and concentrate only on the compatibility or lack of compatibility of the two terms.

Let us say that two terms which can be used together to form significant sentences are U-related terms. To indicate this we prefix the value U to the pair of terms.[1] The U-relation may be defined thus:

$$(X, Y)_i \text{ is not a category mistake} \equiv U(X, Y)_{df}$$
$$(X, Y)_i \text{ is a category mistake} \equiv N(X, Y) \equiv \text{not-}U(X, Y)_{df}.$$

For example, the value for the pair (tall, philosopher) is U and we therefore say: U (philosopher, tall). And if we are given a set of terms—'Socrates', 'philosopher', 'even prime', 'tall', 'fence'— we would write down the following ten values for the pairs: $U(S,P)$, $N(S, E)$, $U(S, T)$, $N(S, F)$, $N(P, E)$, $U(P, T)$, $N(P, F)$, $N(E, T)$, $U(T, F)$, $N(E, F)$.

The properties of the U and N relations form the formal heart of the theory of types. For X and Y to be U-related means that they are significantly conjoinable. And (1) assures us of the symmetry of the U-relation, that is, $U(X, Y) = U(Y, X)$. Clearly the U-relation is also reflexive so that $U(X, X)$ holds for any term in the language. We shall see that one major source of trouble concerns the question whether the U-relation is transitive. But our immediate task is the definition of B-types in terms of the U-relation. This we can now do.

A set of terms S *constitutes a* B-*type of a language if all the terms of* S *are mutually* U-*related so that any pair of terms in* S *has the value* U *and there is no larger set* S′ *in* L *whose terms are mutually* U-*related and such that* S *is included in* S′.

In other words, the B-types of a language are the largest sets of mutually U-related terms. And to say that two terms are of the same B-type is equivalent to saying that they are U-related.

The notion of a set of terms having mutual use may be found in Black as well as in Ryle. It underlies his tentative formulation of a 'negative criterion' for establishing that two expressions are of different types. Black's formulation, like Ryle's, is wider since he

---

[1] The U-relation is defined more elaborately in my paper 'The Ordinary Language Tree'.

intends his criterion to apply to all sorts of expressions, not merely those expressions we here call terms or monadic predicates. But if we confine Black's remarks to terms, we see him making use of the idea of a set of mutually U-related terms. We must, says Black,

interpret the theory of types negatively as essentially an instrument for establishing *differences* of type. . . . The new procedure consists in asserting that two typographically distinct words are syntactically *dissimilar* if there is *at least one* context in which one cannot be substituted for the other without generating nonsense [italics his].[1]

Thus let C be some linguistic context $(\ldots, C)$. We can, says Black, establish that two terms A and B are of different types if we notice that $U(A, C)$ while $N(B, C)$.

Black uses the notion of a mutual U-set of terms for a negative criterion because he does not—as we do—consider mutual U-relatedness to be a sufficient condition for establishing that two terms are of the same type. On our definition of a B-type it is, for example, sufficient to know that U (philosopher, tall) in order for us to say that 'philosopher' and 'tall' belong to the same B-type. But for Black, this is to ignore the fact that U (fence, tall) will also establish that 'tall' and 'fence' are of the same type, and yet we should not wish to go on to say that 'philosopher' and 'fence' are of the same type. For this reason Black ignores the notion of type sameness and uses the notion of mutually U-related terms as a necessary condition for not being of different types.

We may put Black's syntactical criterion symbolically:

$U(X, Y)$ and $N(X, Z)$ implies that Y and Z are of different types.

Black's formula appears to override an important distinction. Look at the following two cases which apply it:

(i) U (Russell, philosopher) and N (prime number, philosopher) implies 'Russell' and 'prime number' are syntactically dissimilar.

(ii) U (Russell, thought about) and N (Russell, continuity) implies that 'thought about' and 'continuity' are syntactically dissimilar.

Does Black wish to consider the type difference in the consequent of (i) to be on a par with the type difference in the consequent of (ii)? The terms of the consequent of (ii) are U-related while the terms of

[1] Black, op. cit., p. 238.

the consequent of (i) are N-related. And if there exists a difference of type between the second two terms, it is quite a different difference from the type difference between the terms of (i).

Yet Black cannot be accused of overlooking the difference between the two cases. For Black denies that the formal type theorist can *have* three terms with the values: $U(X, Y)$, $N(X, Z)$ $U(Y, Z)$. In other words, every time we have $U(X, Y)$ and $N(X, Z)$ this implies that $N(Y, Z)$. Therefore, if we *do* have U (Russell, thought about), N (Russell, continuity), and U (continuity, thought about), *this can only mean* that 'thought about' has *two* senses in its two significant occurrences with 'Russell' and 'continuity'. And in general, if A and B are known to be of different types, then $N(A, B)$:

Thus the application of the theory of types to ordinary language is a more complex undertaking than Russell's own account would suggest. A single attempt at substitution may establish that 'A' is not of the same type as 'B'. Suppose that two sentences are typographically identical except in containing 'A' in place of 'B' then the corresponding symbols, in spite of typographical identity must be considered as belonging to different types.[1]

And this, says Black:

requires the two occurrences of 'thinking' in 'I am thinking about Russell' and 'I am thinking about continuity' to be construed as instances of *two* words belonging to different syntactical types.[2]

Thus Black is not only saying:

(1) $U(X, Y)$ and $N(X, Z)$ implies Y and Z are syntactically dissimilar.

He is also saying:

(2) $U(X, Y)$ and $N(X, Z)$ implies $N(Y, Z)$
or—what is the same thing—
  $U(X, Y)$ and $U(Y, Z)$ implies $U(X, Z)$.

It is because Black maintains (2) that he need not consider case (ii) above. In that case, 'thought about' is equivocal. If it were not equivocal, then we should really say 'I am thinking about continuity' is nonsense. And Russell, too, in his *Reply* agrees with Black in saying that unless 'thought about' is equivocal in the two sentences 'I am

[1] Ibid.
[2] Ibid.

thinking about Russell' and 'I am thinking about continuity', one of these two sentences is nonsensical.[1]

Both Black and Russell, it is clear, consider U to be a *transitive* relation. And Ryle in his paper, *Categories*, also maintains a position which in effect adopts (2) as a syntactical rule. Since these philosophers maintain the rule, it will be necessary to see why they do so. Important philosophical questions turn on its acceptance or rejection. I shall show that the rule must be rejected. But for the moment I wish to show how its acceptance has disastrous consequences for the fourfold distinction of types which has been formulated above. And to do this it will be helpful to introduce an important notion in a formal way, namely 'the use of a term'.

Let $U(X)$ be a set of terms any one of which is U-related to X. We call such a set the 'use of the term X' since it contains all those terms with which X can be paired to form significant sentences. For example, in the set, U (philosopher)—'the use of "philosopher" '— we would have the terms 'philosopher', 'Socrates', 'tall', 'happy', and so on; any term is in its own use since for any term X, it is never the case that $N(X, X)$. Using the notion of the use of a term, we can syntactically define A-types in a convenient way: *a set of terms* S *constitutes an* A-*type in* L *if and only if all the terms of* S *have the same use and there is no larger set* S' *such that all the terms of* S' *have the same use and* S' *includes* S.

The difference between A-types and B-types in the two syntactical definitions may be made clear by considering any two U-related terms X and Y. According to the syntactical formulation of a B-type it is clear that: $U(X, Y) \equiv X$ and Y are of the same B-type. On the other hand, given $U(X, Y)$, we do *not* know that X and Y are of the same A-type. For it may be that there is a term Z such that $U(X, Z)$ and $N(Y, Z)$, or such that $U(Y, Z)$ and $N(X, Z)$. If there is, then the use of X will not be the same as the use of Y.

But now, if the transitivity rule (2) holds, it follows that there can *never* be such a term Z, since $U(X, Y)$ and $U(Y, Z)$ always implies that $U(X, Z)$ and, similarly, $U(X, Y)$ and $U(X, Z)$ implies $U(Y, Z)$. In short, for any two terms X and Y, $U(X, Y) \equiv X$ and Y are of the same A-type, and the distinction between A- and B-types is obliterated in favour of the former. A-types as we defined them are indeed transitive with respect to type sameness. But for those who maintain the transitivity of the U-relation, B-types, like A-types, become tran-

[1] Ibid., p. 691.

sitive, and indeed there is no meaning any longer to the distinction between the two kinds of types. Since this undercuts the whole principle underlying the fourfold distinction of types, it will be necessary to deal the formula (2) a decisive blow. It is not an over-statement to say that the adoption of (2) as a syntactical rule is responsible for the lack of an adequate type theory for natural languages. Black, using the rule, comes to the conclusion that any formal type theory for natural languages leads to ever finer differences and shades of meaning which one would never wish to make, a *reductio ad absurdum* for any attempt to apply formal techniques to natural languages. For whenever we come across a triad of sentences— $U(X, Y)$, $U(X, Z)$, $N(Y, Z)$—we are forced to split the meaning of X in order to avoid violating the transitivity rule. We saw this happen for 'thought about' in the case of U (Russell, thought about), U (continuity, thought about), N (Russell, continuity).

The consistent elaboration of this leading idea involves the making of ever finer distinctions of 'meaning' between words not customarily regarded as ambiguous.[1]

The source of all the difficulties, Black believes, is to be found in the Russell programme itself. Formal techniques, techniques which seek the structure of arguments without regard to meaning but with strict regard to rules and substitution possibilities, ought not to be applied to natural language, or at any rate ought to be applied only 'on occasion':

The demonstration of distinctions of type, defined in terms of mutual substitution of words, is on occasion a valuable technique for exhibiting operative ambiguity whose removal is relevant for the solution of philo-sophical disputes. But the consequences of an attempt to apply such techniques universally may be regarded as a *reductio ad absurdum* of a point of view which seeks to apply to ordinary language segregatory criteria appropriate to an artificially constructed calculus. And this in turn can be traced back to the inclination to regard the relation between the world and language exclusively in the light of identity of structure.[2]

The idea that a logical 'formal' correction of natural language can be ontologically revealing is central to the Russell programme. So far as a theory of types is concerned, Black's use of the transitivity principle leads to a principled scepticism about the possibility of

[1] Black, op. cit., p. 239.
[2] Ibid., p. 240.

such a formal ontology. But may it not be the case that this *reductio* ought to be turned on itself? It is, after all, the rule of transitivity which leads into scepticism. This reflects on this 'rule', not on the search for a rule. It is because Black, Russell, Ryle, and others have unquestioningly accepted the assumption that any 'theory' of types requires that type sameness must be transitive, that formal type theory has so far been futile. If Ryle and Black have turned to 'informal logic' using 'techniques' only on the proper occasions (but when is an occasion proper?) it is because they have found the transitivity of the U-relation too strong an assumption. And if Russell is reduced to a hope for a good theory of types, and to the lame acceptance of the 'ever finer distinctions' which Black has shown to be required, this too is due to his unquestioning acceptance of the transitivity rule. We are thus left with only two alternatives. Accept the unwelcome consequences and make all the fine distinctions called for by the use of the rule, or drop the attempt to use formal techniques for natural languages.

It is evident that we need a type theory which does not lead to the making of counter-intuitive distinctions of sense, a theory which dispenses with the rule of transitivity as a formal type rule, yet one which uses a formal type rule and applies it *universally* to natural language. But first we ought to see why philosophers have been seduced by the transitivity rule to such an extent that they did not believe in the possibility of any type theory which dispenses with it.

A serious reason appears legitimately to dictate the acceptance of transitivity for the U-relation. In any natural language it is possible to formulate interesting and sometimes funny sorts of Rylean sentences known as zeugmas. Examples are 'She came home in a sedan chair and a flood of tears', 'The chair and question were hard', 'Some periods are punctuation marks while others are vacations'. Each of the two sentences 'The chair is hard' and 'The question is hard' is significant, yet 'The chair and the question were hard' is a category mistake. If we assume transitivity, this becomes quite clear: we have U (chair, hard) and U (question, hard), while N (question, chair). Since that would violate transitivity, we are *forced* to say that 'hard' has two senses in those two sentences. Thus the transitivity rule shows us that 'hard' must have two senses. And for this reason the sentence 'The chair and question are hard' is a category mistake. In a *single* sentence, we have no opportunity to make the necessary distinction called for by the use of the transitivity rule.

One tempting way to avoid accepting the transitivity rule to account for zeugmas must be stoutly resisted by the formalist: he may not say that the ambiguity in 'hard' is not known by means of a rule. He cannot appeal to the 'obviousness' of the equivocation. If he does that he gives the case away to the informalist. Thus he is apparently presented with the dilemma which confronted Russell: accept the transitivity rule and you generate ambiguity where you don't want it, or reject transitivity and you fail to account for it where you ought to. The case of U (hard, chair), U (hard, question), N (question, chair) is an example of the second sort. The case of U (Russell, thought about), U (continuity, thought about), N (Russell, continuity) is an example of the first sort.

The fact that zeugmas suggest the transitivity principle is not overlooked by Ryle. He uses the principle to establish that 'exist' has several senses in its use with 'prime numbers' and 'Wednesdays' and 'navies'.

A man would be thought to be making a poor joke who said that three things are now rising, namely, the tide, hopes, and the average age of death. It would be just as good or bad a joke to say that there exist prime numbers and Wednesdays and public opinions and navies; or that there exist both bodies and minds.[1]

Ryle is arguing that 'exists' cannot univocally be used with prime numbers and navies because they are of different types. And just as N (hopes, tides), U (hopes, rising), and U (tides, rising) 'shows' us that 'rising' is equivocal, so too N (prime numbers, navies), U (exist, navies), and U (exist, prime numbers) 'show' us that 'exists' is equivocal. The existence of zeugmas, in short, is supposed to indicate to us that there can be no three terms X, Y, and Z such that $U(X, Y)$, $U(X, Z)$ and $N(Y, Z)$. Yet Ryle himself uses this principle only 'as a valuable technique for exhibiting operative ambiguity whose removal is relevant to the solution of philosophical problems'; he does so only 'on occasion'. It is Ryle who coined the phrase 'informal logic'.

Anyone using the transitivity principle 'on occasion' is bound to use it in an informal spirit. The consequences of applying it universally are, as Black has shown, too severe. Yet a technique which is applicable only on occasion for 'exhibiting operative ambiguity' cannot be employed to enforce ambiguity in those cases where it is in doubt. And surely the ambiguity or univocity of 'exists' is here in doubt.

[1] Ryle, *The Concept of Mind* (New York, 1949), p. 23.

Unless both Black and Ryle are prepared to employ their technique universally—which in view of the unwelcome consequences they are not—they cannot do more than account for the zeugmatic character of *known* zeugmas; the informalist spirit oversteps its bounds when it attempts to enforce a judgement of zeugma on a dubious case. Indeed, the whole idea of using a logical technique only in certain cases (however obvious and 'operative'), and refraining from using it in others, is quite inadmissible. It is as much of a *reductio* as the unwelcome consequences which threaten us when we seek to apply the transitivity rule universally. But it may be that I have not yet caught the full spirit of this approach.

In any case, we have before us three alternatives: (1) Use the transitivity rule 'on occasion', for example, in accounting for 'obvious' zeugmas. (2) Accept transitivity and face the 'unwelcome consequences' of generating ambiguity in counter-intuitive instances. (3) Reject transitivity and face the consequences of being unable to account even for obvious zeugmas. The first way is adopted by those who despair of the second two formalistic alternatives. Black and Ryle are its representatives. The formalist must reject it or surrender to Black's criticism. It is interesting that Russell, like Ryle, stoutly maintains that existence is equivocal. And of course he is forced to say this if he accepts transitivity in the formal spirit. On the other hand, any formalistic philosopher who maintains that existence is univocal is forced to accept the third alternative. A striking and belligerent case is Quine.

Quine, for well-known reasons of his own, rejects Ryle's and Russell's view that 'existence' is equivocal, and with his usual boldness he does not shirk the consequences. For if we insist on the univocity of existence, we thereby deprive ourselves of the use of the transitivity assumption to enforce ambiguity. Since Quine does not wish to employ the transitivity rule for existence (for example, for ambiguity in the sentences 'chair exists' and 'question exists'), he cannot avail himself of this rule for 'hard' either.

Why not say that chairs and questions, however unlike, are hard in a single inclusive sense of the word? There is an air of zeugma about 'The chair and question were hard' but is it not due merely to the dissimilarity of chairs and questions? Are we not in effect calling 'hard' ambiguous if at all, just because it is true of some very unlike things?

* * *

Essentially this same question comes up in instances that are taken seriously. There are philosophers who stoutly maintain that 'true' said of logical or mathematical laws and 'true' said of weather predictions or suspects' confessions are two usages of an ambiguous term 'true'. There are philosophers who stoutly maintain that 'exists' said of numbers, classes, and the like, and 'exists' said of material objects are two usages of an ambiguous term 'exists'. What mainly baffles me is the stoutness of their maintenance. What can they possibly count as evidence? Why not view 'true' as unambiguous but very general, and recognize the difference between true logical laws and true confessions as a difference merely between logical laws and confessions? And correspondingly for existence?[1]

Having ruled out the transitivity rule as a method for enforcing a judgement of ambiguity, Quine finds 'no evidence' for calling 'existence' and 'truth' and 'hard' ambiguous when predicated of things of different types. But the evidence for the rule appears clear enough. The *Oxford English Dictionary* gives us an example of a zeugma: 'She came home in a flood of tears and a bath chair'. If the rule of transitivity is rejected why is that a zeugma? Why not say that 'what she came home in' has a single general sense which applies univocally to bath chairs and floods of tears? Indeed, all so-called zeugmas can be treated in the way Quine suggests. The existence of zeugmas *suggests* the rule of transitivity. Zeugmas appear incorrect because they embody an allegedly univocal use of a term in a way which violates the rule of transitivity. If Quine rejects the transitivity rule he is faced with the question 'Why is "hard" univocal while "what she came home in" is not?' He evidently does not wish to validate *all* zeugmas; he must therefore supply some criterion for distinguishing between ambiguous and univocal predicates that are used with things of different types. On such a criterion, it should turn out that 'hard' is ambiguous while 'exists' need not be. We shall later see that this is indeed the case. On any such criterion, 'what she came home in' ought to turn out to be ambiguous.

Quine is in fact correct in ruling out the transitivity rule as a method for enforcing ambiguity. But since the existence of zeugmas apparently suggests the existence of a transitivity rule, we are left with the two intolerable 'formalist' alternatives: accept the transitivity rule and enforce ambiguity in words 'not customarily regarded as ambiguous', or reject the rule and find 'no evidence' for enforcing distinctions in words that are not customarily regarded as univocal. I shall confine myself now to showing that the rule must be rejected.

[1] Quine, op. cit., pp. 130–131.

Another rule, to be stated later, supplies the needed criterion which takes us between the horns of the dilemma.

III

Is it in fact a rule that for any three univocal expressions, $U(X, Y)$ and $U(X, Z)$ implies $U(Y, Z)$? To show, on *purely formal* grounds, that this *cannot* be a rule is the task now before us.

The 'grounds', however, consist of answers to two important questions which have not been explicitly considered by most philosophers of natural language. We speak very often of a term as being a term of a given language. It is obvious that in order for a given term T to be part of a language L, it must have some use in L. Furthermore, if every sentence containing T were a category mistake, then, though T had grammatical use, it could not be considered as a part of the language L. Or at any rate, it would have no 'meaning' in L, and we are concerned with the meaningful terms of L. Thus our first question is: what use conditions must a term fulfil in order to have meaning in (be a term of) a given language? And our answer to this question must be that it is at least a necessary condition that T be U-related to at least one other expression of L, in order for T to be in L. We shall need no more than the knowledge of this necessary condition for our purpose.

But a second question immediately poses itself: what conditions of *mutual* use must a *set* of terms fulfil in order that the set be the terms of a given language? For example, we often say that a given group of predicates is in the *same* language as another group. What (besides purely grammatical rules which allow for substitutions) use conditions hold for this? A formal restatement, employing the 'U-relation', will enable us to deal with this question.

We consider a model natural language NL containing terms A, B, $C \ldots K$. Any pair of these terms will have a sense value (U or N) depending on whether the terms in the pair are U-related or not. Since this is a natural language some of the pairs will be N in value. Thus if $A = $ 'angry', $B = $ 'bold', $C = $ 'crime', $D = $ 'drowsy', we might have values $U(A, B)$, $N(C, D)$, $U(B, C)$, and so forth.

The use condition already stated requires that the sense values for the pairs of terms of NL must be such that every term appear at least once in a pair which has the value U. But now suppose that the use condition is met with the following values for the terms of NL, all other pairs except those listed having the value N.

(1) $U(A, B), U(A, C), U(C, D), U(E, F), U(E, G),$
             $U(E, H), U(E, I), U(E, J), U(E, K).$

Given these values, every term has some use with at least one other term of NL. We notice, however, that the language may be divided in two since none of the terms A, B, C, D has any connexion in use with any of the terms of the set E, F, G, H, I, J, K. So far as their use with one another is concerned we have indeed no reason to consider the first group of terms to be in the same language with the second group. Thus the answer to our second question is that for a set of terms to be terms of the *same* language, it is a necessary condition that all the terms of the set be connected through mutual use with one another. This does not mean that all of them must be mutually U-related with one another. The fact that we have the value $N(B, C)$ does not mean that B and C are not connected. Their connexion may be assured by the U-values for the pairs (A, B) and (A, C). Thus the terms of the subset A, B, C, D are connected with one another but they are all unconnected with the terms of the second group. To be part of a language is to have some use. To be a group of terms in the same language is to have connected use.

The connectedness condition may be more formally stated. Using '$con(X, Y)$' to mean the X and Y are in the same language, the following two relations hold:

  (i) $U(X, Y)$ and $U(X, Z)$ implies $con(Y, Z)$.
  (ii) $con(Y, Z)$ and $con(W, Z)$ implies $con(Y, W)$.

We can now say that if a set of terms $A, B, C \ldots K$ are terms of the same language, then any two of them are connected through the use of the terms in the language. The values given in (1) above do not assure the connectedness of all the terms. If we changed the value of (B, J) from N to U, however, all the terms would then be connected.

The two conditions just stated—the use condition for a *single* term to be in a given language and the connectedness condition for a *group* of terms to be terms of the *same* language—are fundamental. I shall refer to them as linguistic conditions since no language *is* a language unless it satisfies them. They are, of course, only necessary conditions, but they suffice for our immediate purposes.

We are now assuming that every natural language is *connected through use*. But now let us suppose that sameness of type is transitive. This, we recall, is (2): for any three terms X, Y, and Z, $U(X, Y)$ and $U(X, Z)$ implies $U(Y, Z)$. Since the language is connected, (2) would enable us to prove that any two terms are U-related. For example, suppose our language contained only four terms and the values $U(A, B)$,

$U(A, C)$, $U(B, C)$, $U(C, D)$, $N(A, D)$, $N(B, D)$. These values satisfy the linguistic conditions of the use and connectedness. But now by applying (2) we could show that (A, D) and (B, D) must *also* be U since $U(A, C)$ and $U(C, D)$ implies $U(A, D)$, and $U(A, D)$ and $U(A, B)$ implies $U(B, D)$. In other words, for any connected language, the use of the transitivity rule insures that *all* possible pairs of the language are U in value. But this means that the language contains no type mistakes and hence *no type distinctions*. The very meaning of the sense value U is obliterated if there can be no pairs with the value N. Thus we have shown that any connected language containing type distinctions (that is, *any natural language*) cannot use (2) to enforce distinctions of sense. The transitivity rule is, therefore, not a possible rule for a natural language.

We noted the dilemma in which we are placed by the lack of a rule of transitivity for type sameness. Without this rule, which we have now found to be contralinguistic, we can have $U(A, B)$, $U(A, C)$, and $N(B, C)$, and when we do, we have no warrant for a judgement of ambiguity for the term A. Quine and others who maintain that 'exists' is univocal in the pairs (chair, exists) and (question, exists) are thereby free to hold this position. But we noted also the price they pay. We do need an ambiguity rule. Quine says that 'hard', too, is univocal in (chair, hard) and (question, hard). He finds 'no evidence' for a judgement of ambiguity. But this can go too far. There is also no evidence for a judgement of ambiguity in the pairs (period, vacation) and (period, smudged), no evidence for ambiguity in (rational, number) and (rational, man) and in general no evidence for the ambiguity of *any* term that has heterotypical uses.

Though the transitivity rule is unavailable, this does not mean we cannot find some *other formal* way of proving ambiguity. It must be acknowledged that Quine's request for 'evidence' is quite legitimate. Any term is univocal until proven equivocal. But what sort of proof is appropriate? The correct answer to this question is of fundamental importance.

One basic requirement for any criterion for enforcing a judgement of ambiguity is that the criterion enable us to do this *whether or not we understand the meaning or meanings of the term* in question. Indeed, we cannot be said to know the meaning of a term whose univocity is in question. Thus it must be possible to show that the term has two meanings (or more) and to show that this is so *whatever the term may mean*. A criterion which requires a knowledge of the meaning or meanings of the term is not admissible. Those who approach philosophy in the ordinary language spirit, with no more than a better

than average intuitive discernment of the nuances and senses of the
terms they wish to analyse or clarify, are bound to violate this fundamental requirement. Philosophy, in large part, is the technique of
making important and needed distinctions of sense for crucial terms.
For this reason it is necessary to be clear about what happens when
clarifying distinctions are made. Problems about the logic of clarification are as old as Plato's *Meno* and as recent as the so-called paradox
of analysis. In the attempt to be clear about clarification, the spirit
of the Russell programme is a far better guide than the 'informalist'
spirit of the later Wittgenstein. Any clarification procedure, any
logical procedure for showing that a given expression has different
meanings in two or more of its occurrences, ought, ideally, to be one
which enforces those distinctions in a truly logical way, that is,
independently of the 'meaning' or 'meanings' the particular expression may have. Moreover, the Russell spirit demands that we
consider a term to be thus equivocal *for no other reason* than the fact
that a given clarification rule *requires* that the term has two senses and
not one. If one cannot prove a term to be equivocal, it is not equivocal.
We never merely discern it to be. This is only another way of saying
that ambiguity is not a fact in language; it is the result of the application of a 'clarification procedure'. There is no such fact as ambiguity
which the procedure enables us to discern. It is the procedure which
forces us to consider an expression ambiguous. And it does so independently of the 'meanings' we then discern.

By a clarification procedure I mean a procedure which we use
implicitly or explicitly to detect a meaning distinction or, better, to
enforce a judgement that an expression which recurs in two or more
contexts has more than one meaning. The *whole* context containing the
recurrent expression I shall call a linguistic sequence. A sequence may
be a sentence or longer.

A linguistic sequence may be correct or incorrect in different ways.
I shall consider three such ways by way of illustrating the general
character of clarification. A sequence may be grammatical or ungrammatical, it may be category correct or category mistaken, it may
be consistent or inconsistent. We may call these ways of being correct
or incorrect 'levels of rectitude'. The reason for calling them levels
is that a sequence which is incorrect in one way must be correct in
other ways and the ways it must be correct are therefore 'lower' than,
because presupposed by, the way it is incorrect. Also, an incorrect
sequence is neither correct nor incorrect with respect to other ways,
and these ways are 'higher' since they presuppose the rectitude of the

sequence. For example, an ungrammatical sentence is not a sentence at all; it cannot therefore make a category mistake. Thus the incorrectness we call a category mistake presupposes the grammaticalness of the sentence. Again, a category mistake is neither consistent nor inconsistent. If I say 'his anger was triangular and not triangular' I have not contradicted myself; I have said nothing and retracted nothing. An inconsistent sentence is neither true nor false empirically. Thus inconsistency as a way of being incorrect presupposes both the grammaticalness *and* the category correctness of the sequence. Again, empirical falsity presupposes that the sequence is grammatical, category correct, *and* consistent. In short, any sequence which is incorrect at one level of rectitude must be correct at all lower levels and is neither correct nor incorrect at any higher level.

A given sequence contains ambiguity if and only if:

> (a) it is incorrect at some level of rectitude if all terms are taken univocally;
> (b) there are pragmatic reasons to consider the sequence to be correct at that level;
> (c) the sequence is correct if some recurrent expression is treated as if it were nonrecurrent.

Consider a sequence which violates grammatical rules. A foreigner who knows very little English hears someone say 'I peer at the peer'. This sentence sounds ungrammatical (a) since if 'peer' has only one meaning the sentence lacks a verb phrase. Since he hears the sequence spoken by a native speaker he has reason to consider it grammatically correct (b). He therefore doctors the sentence and says to himself (as it were): 'Whatever this word 'peer' means, it has two meanings in this sentence. In its first occurrence it is a verb, in its second it is a noun'.

The clarification procedure involved here does not require a knowledge of the meaning of the term judged to be ambiguous. The procedure can be applied to any similar case (I x the x., for example, 'I saw the saw', and so forth).

We have so far no clarification procedure for the category level of rectitude. The discarded transitivity rule, however, is the *sort* of thing we want. With that rule one need not know the meaning of the word 'period' to declare it ambiguous in the sequence 'the period was my vacation'. . . . 'The period was smudged'. All one needs to know is the fact that (vacation, smudged) cannot be used together. If we have any reason to accept the sentences embodying 'period' as category correct, we could then use the transitivity rule to doctor them, giving 'period' two meanings. This rule, however, is now unavailable to us. We have therefore to look for something *like* the transitivity rule which can do the job we need done. The new rule and its use as a clarification procedure will be presently illustrated.

Inconsistency is a common enforcer of ambiguity. If I hear someone say 'It is raining and it isn't' I recognize a violation of inconsistency (a). I nevertheless have good reason to consider the sentence consistent (b). I therefore construe the sentence with two meanings of 'raining' (c). In connection with inconsistency as a clarification procedure, it is worth noting that there are probably no tautologies in ordinary language. When someone says 'Boys will be boys', 'War is war', 'What will be will be', 'Business is business', it is always acceptable to deny the statement and then to use inconsistency to enforce the ambiguity intended in the original assertion.

A clarification procedure is nothing but a language rule applied in a certain way. Any language rule, when it is violated, can be used in one of two ways. (1) We can throw out the offending sequence, or (2) we can use the rule to introduce ambiguity in such a way that the rule is no longer violated by the sequence. In artificial languages the rules are used only in the first way; in natural languages we often use a rule to 'clarify'. It is sometimes said by those favouring constructed languages that the natural language is shot through with ambiguity because it is anarchical, not governed by rules. The opposite is true; the ambiguity is a product of the rules. It is due to their satisfaction.

Enough has now been said about clarification procedures as such. In what follows, a rule for the category 'level of rectitude' will be stated and a proof of the rule will be offered. Its application for clarification will then be illustrated.

IV

The main object of the ensuing analysis is to tie together several seemingly disparate topics. These include: (a) a theory of types (that is, a theory describing the *way* terms are conjoined to form category correct statements in a natural language); (b) a formal theory of ontological categories and ontological features; (c) a theory of *predication* (that is, a theory accounting for the subject-predicate distinction and one which provides certain formal characteristics of the binary relation 'is predicable of'); (d) a procedure for enforcing ambiguity.

The results of the analysis support the main features of the Russell programme. I take these to be that (a) clarification of natural language is ontologically revealing and discriminatory of the sorts of things there are; (b) linguistic structures and ontological structures are isomorphic. The meaning of 'ontology' in what immediately follows is 'the science of categories'.

We have noted that whenever a predicate P is significantly applicable to a thing, then so is its complement non-P. Now this gives us the right to treat predicates as having no 'sign' *for purposes of a type analysis*. Thus, any predicate P can be construed as $|P|$ or 'the absolute value' of P, by which we mean that P spans the things that are either P or non-P but does not span things which are neither P nor non-P. For example, if P = philosopher, then $|P|$ defines the class of things which are either philosophers or nonphilosophers. In the class of things that are $|P|$ are Bertrand Russell and Cleopatra but not the Empire State Building. Henceforth I shall call a class defined by an absolute predicate an *ontological* class or *category*. If we use the terminology introduced above, α-types are *categories*.

Apparently, anything whatever belongs to the category of things that are |thought about|, |interesting|, or |discussed at the Aristotelian society|. Also in a most general sense of the term (the sense preferred by Quine) anything whatsoever belongs to the category of things that |exists|.

To say of something that it |exists| or that it is |interesting| is to give no information whatsoever about the nature of the thing. For this reason, some philosophers have chosen to consider such categories trivial. On the other hand, to say of something that it is a |philosopher| does tell us something; we know at least that it is the sort of thing which is |angry| or a |citizen of the United States| and that it is not |prime| and not |valid|, and the like. It is evident that many absolute predicates define the same categories. Thus |interesting| and |discussed| define a single category, and so do |angry| and |sad|. This fact corresponds to our A-types since an A-type consists of a set of predicates which span the same things. By absolutizing the predicates of any given A-type, we merely cut the number of predicates in that type by half.

Indeed, just as we can reduce the two predicates 'philosopher' and 'nonphilosopher' to one predicate $|P|$, so can we reduce *all* of the predicates of a given A-type to one single absolute predicate, since they are all 'synonymous'. To say that a thing is |angry| is to say no more but also no less than that it is |sad| or |alert|. The language of ontology is a bare skeleton of ordinary language, and for its purposes we require only *one* absolute predicate from each A-type; we can ignore all the synonyms. Each A-type defines a category (or α-type) and a single absolute predicate from the A-type defines the same category; for ontological purposes we could make do with that single one.

If now we take an ordinary language and absolutize all of its predicates so that instead of being able to say that a thing is P we could say only that it is $|P|$ we could then give only *ontological information*. Imagine a 'Twenty Questions' game in which the player has something in mind for us to guess (it could be a valid argument or a bumblebee). And imagine that in asking the questions, we are permitted to use only absolute predicates. It is evident that we could never get enough information to specify the individual thing he has in mind. All we could do is determine the *sort* of thing it is. We might ask whether the thing is |interesting| but that would be a wasted question. We might ask whether it is |red| and if the answer were yes, we would know that he has nothing like a valid argument in mind, but something physical. Following that it would be a waste to ask further whether the thing is |green|. We might then ask whether it is |kind| and an affirmative answer to that would inform us that it is not a pebble or a tree or an inanimate object but that it is the sort of thing which is either kind or not, and so on. We could not get to distinguish the thing but we could get its ontological type in this way (more precisely, we could get its β-type). The category language is embedded in every natural language. To expose it, all we need to do is absolutize the predicates. A language of absolute predicates is a purely ontological language. And every natural language has its ontological skeleton, its 'ontology.'

The *ontologist* is interested in categories; he is, *qua* ontologist, not interested in whether a thing is red or whether it is green but in whether it is coloured. Even this is not altogether accurate: he is interested in its character of being coloured or colourless. For the ontologist 'coloured' means |red| which is the same thing as coloured or colourless. A toothache is neither, but water can be either red or not red or coloured or colourless.

We speak as ontologists when, for example, we say that points belong to the category of extension even though they belong to the *class* of extensionless things. The category of extension is defined by the predicate |extended| and points belong to it.[1] Concepts do not belong to it since they are neither extended nor extensionless. Space (spatial) is another category word since it has no complement which is not categorial. And if the word 'colour' is taken to include that 'colour' we call 'colourless', it too is a category word. There are quite a few words which can be taken *either* in their absolute sense as category words or in their class sense. Thus 'exists', if taken as a category word, has no opposite. 'Exists' then is the same as |exists|. The confusions from the discussion in Plato's *Sophist* to this day over the use of 'exists' as a category or a class word are dispelled once we take care to keep the absolute or categorial meaning of 'exists' separate from its ordinary predicate meaning. The *class* of things which do not exist belong to the *category* of existence. Flute-playing centaurs belong to the former by virtue of the fact that they belong to the latter. I could call a horse a flute-playing centaur and I would be mistaken since there are no flute-playing centaurs, but in this respect I am at least mistaken, something I would not be if I called the horse a prime number. The class of things that do not exist is limited to what we can mistakenly say does exist. A horse which is a prime number neither exists nor does not exist. But in saying that I predicate nothing of horses, I merely say that the category of existence is the ontology of the language as given by the absolute predicates of the language. 'A horse which is a prime number' is not in the language, and neither is 'round anger'. Predicates that are not in the language cannot be used to say anything and we must perforce 'be silent'. The absolute predicate |is spoken of| defines the category of things that can be spoken of, a category which is coextensive with that of existence. But 'cannot be spoken of', like 'inexistent', is an illegitimate complement to an *absolute* predicate. Ramsey's remark that you can't whistle it either is the satirical remark of a discerning ontologist.

An absolute predicate defines a class of things but, like any ordinary predicate, it does so by singling out what the members of the class have in common. I shall use the word 'property' to refer to what the members of a class defined by a predicate have in common. What the members of an *ontological* class, or category, defined by an

---

[1] Not all ontologists are alive to this. Thus Whitehead considers it a *problem* that points—being extensionless—are in the category of extension, and he develops a method for defining them in terms of extended things. Descartes is properly unworried about this.

absolute predicate have in common I shall call a *feature*. Thus the predicate 'red' defines a category which has a certain feature. There is no word to locate this feature unless we take colour to locate the attribute of either having some colour or being colourless. A paraphrase is 'the red-or-nonredness' of a thing. Whether one interprets absolute predicates as locating categories or whether one interprets them as locating category features is a matter of indifference to the ontologist and should be a matter of indifference to the logician. Any logical laws which apply to absolute predicates will take either interpretation.

Are any features or categories of greater interest to the ontologist than others? One suspects, for example, that the category of existence is of greater ontological interest than the category of colour. There are two sorts of categories which are of major importance to ontologists. These are the categories which are all inclusive, containing all others as subcategories, and those that are completely exclusive, containing no subcategories at all. Thus when Russell chose the predicate 'philosopher', he was choosing one of the latter categories since no absolute predicate in the language defines a category of things included in the one defined by 'philosopher'.

We have as yet no right to assume that there must be categories of these two types. The existence of categories which include all others may be denied and is denied by those who say, for example, that 'exists' does not span things of different types univocally. To be sure, they have 'no evidence' for this since the transitivity rule is, as we saw, linguistically impossible. On the other hand, so long as we have no rule to enforce ambiguity, we have no assurance that 'exists' and other terms such as 'is thought about' are of the highest level. Such terms, if they *are* univocal, are U-related to all other terms and we need a proof for their existence in the language.

Nor do we have formal assurance of the existence of lowest-level categories, categories which include no others. For it could even be that categories merely overlap in membership and that no categories include others, though some perhaps are coextensive.

The existence of dominating categories and categories of the lowest level is however assured by a fundamental law which governs all categories. This law can be derived from a 'syntactical' rule governing the distribution of category correct statement in a natural language. Equally, the rule can be derived from the law. Indeed the law of categories and the law governing the distribution of category mistakes are two expressions of a structural isomorphism which holds between 'language' and 'ontology'. In its categorial form, the structural principle may be thus expressed:

> If C_1 and C_2 are any two categories, then either C_1 and C_2 have no members in common or $\mathbf{C}_1$ is included in $\mathbf{C}_2$ or $\mathbf{C}_2$ is included in C_1.

Given this law and the already noted fact that the categories (α-types) defined by the predicates of any natural language are finite in number, it will follow that there must be one category that includes all others and several that include no others.

I shall call this the law of categorial inclusion since it states that whenever two categories have some common membership, one of the two is included in the other. In terms of 'features' the law of categorial inclusion asserts that for any features F_1 and F_2 which characterize some given object, it is either the case that all objects possessing F_1 also possess F_2 or vice versa. In what follows, the symbol $|\,P\,|$ will be used for the absolute predicate *or* for the category which it defines. No serious harm is done by this double use; it is analogously traditional to use the same symbol for a class term and for the class it defines. The law of categorial inclusion may, accordingly, be formulated in three equivalent ways:

$$(\text{T.1}) \; U(P\,Q) \equiv \left[(|P| \subset |Q| \vee (|Q| \subset |P|) \right]$$
$$U(P\,Q) \equiv (x)\,(|P|_x \supset |Q|_x) \vee (x)\,(|Q|_x \supset |P|_x)$$
$$U(P\,Q) \equiv (x)\left[(x\epsilon|P|) \supset (x\epsilon|Q|) \right] \vee (x)\left[(x\epsilon|Q|) \supset (x\epsilon|P|) \right]$$

The proof of this law is given in an appendix to this paper. An important theorem that is derivable from T.1 holds for any three terms P, Q, and R:

$$(\text{T.2}) \; \frac{U(P,\,Q)\,U(Q,\,R)\,N(P,\,R) \equiv (|P| \subset |Q|)\,(|R| \subset |Q|)}{(|Q| \subset |P|)\,(|Q| \subset |R|)\,(|P| \subset |R|)\,(|R| \subset |P|)}$$

The importance of T.2 lies in its clear statement of an equivalence between syntactical and categorial relations, between sense and non-sense gotten by conjoining terms, and the inclusions among the sets of things they span. From another side, T.2 states a simple criterion which validates the subject-predicate distinction. To see this clearly, let us substitute the symbol '$\rightarrow$' wherever we have the inclusion symbol '$\subset$' and let us interpret '$Q \leftarrow P$' to mean: 'of (what is) P it is significant to say that it is Q'. Or—what is the same thing—'that it is Q' is *predicable* of (what is) P. We now have

$$\frac{U(X,\,Y)\,U(X,\,Z)\,N(Y,\,Z)}{\equiv (X \leftarrow Y)\,(X \leftarrow Z)\,(Y \leftarrow X)\,(Z \leftarrow X)\,(Y \leftarrow Z)\,(Z \leftarrow Y)}$$

This tells us that the middle term X of two significant pairs (sentences) is always the predicate with respect to the two N-related terms Y and Z of a triad, $U(X, Y) \ U(X, Z) \ N(Y, Z)$. The relational expression 'is predicable of' is thus seen to be isomorphic with the relational expression 'contains'. Both the relations of predication and of containment are *transitive* and *nonsymmetrical*. In this respect *the predicative tie between terms differs from the tie of significance or U-relatedness since the U-relation is, as we have seen, nontransitive and symmetrical.*

Aristotle always insisted on the metaphor of inclusion for 'predication'; a paradigm for predication was saying of a species that it was included in a genus. The metaphor fails, if taken literally, in most cases. Thus Aristotle also insisted that being a man could not be predicated of what was white, but because he failed to make a clear distinction between class and category he could not rightly see why this was so. The criterion of inclusion works for categories but not for classes. For such cases Aristotle used a special theory of substance and attribute to ground the subject-predicate distinction. But 'being human' is no less an attribute of a thing than being white, and most recent philosophers have rightly deplored the use of a special ontological doctrine to account for the subject-predicate distinction. It is nevertheless illegitimate to proceed from a repudiation of the substance-attribute distinction to a repudiation of the subject-predicate distinction. We do not, in fact, need the 'substantival'-'adjectival' dichotomy with its metaphysical trappings for the subject-predicate distinction. We can just as easily show that in the pair (white, human) 'human' is the subject term and 'white' is the predicate term, as we could show that 'man' is the subject term in the pair (man, white). All we need is the UUN triad and a third term such that U (white, x) and N (human, x). The term 'sky' will do. Thus the view set forth in this essay supports the Aristotelian insistence on the nonsymmetry of predication[1] and does so for much the same reasons—the inclusion of *categories*. In having insisted on the substance-attribute theory for the nonsymmetry of predication, Aristotle was wrong. But he is less wrong than those who—in fear of metaphysical interference in pure logic—have abandoned the subject-predicate distinction altogether.[2]

[1] For the view that predication is symmetrical see F. P. Ramsey's 'Universals', *The Foundations of Mathematics* (London and New York, 1931), pp. 116 ff.

[2] P. F. Strawson in *Individuals* (London, 1959), pp. 167 ff., uses a 'category' criterion to defend the traditional distinction of subject and predicate. But his notion of 'category' is not mine.

A third theorem that follows from the law of categorial inclusion is purely syntactical. I have elsewhere called this theorem 'the tree rule' since it distributes the monadic predicate terms of a language on the 'nodes' of a hierarchical tree for purposes of allowing for conjoining them significantly and exhibiting which pairs of them are copredicable. T.3 can also be used to enforce distinctions of sense for certain expressions whose relations of cosignificance and lack of cosignificance is assumed to be known. T.3 is easily derivable from T.2. It holds for any four terms P, Q, R and S.

(T.3) $\sim \big[U(P\,Q)\, U(QR)\, U(PS)\, N(PR)\, N(QS) \big]$

Proof: $U(P\,Q)\, U(QR)\, N(PR) \supset (|P| \subset |Q|)$ by T.2

                      $U(P\,Q)\, U(PS)\, N(QS) \supset (|Q| \subset |P|)$ by T.2

$\therefore \quad \sim \big[U(P\,Q)\, U(QR)\, U(PS)\, N(PR)\, N(QS) \big]$ $Q.E.D.$

If (A, B) is some significant subject-predicate sentence of the sort, say, that normally occurs in syllogistic argument, then the tree rule states that whatever makes sense with A makes sense with B, *or* whatever makes sense with B makes sense with A. Thus we cannot have $U(AB)$ $U(AC)\, N(BC)$ and *also* $U(AB)\, U(BD)\, N(AD)$.

If we keep the arrow notation we can conveniently represent how the tree rule distributes the terms of the natural language into (a) relative positions for category correct predication and (b) B-types and A-types.

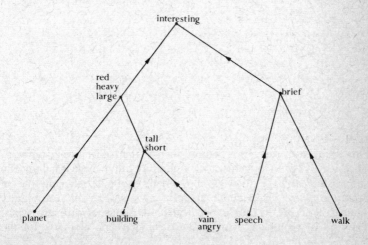

For an illustration we may use a 'model natural language'. There are five 'roots' to the tree for that 'language', corresponding to the number of its *B*-types. A *B*-type consists of a set of terms along a permitted path. Thus 'interesting', 'brief', 'walk' is a *B*-type. There are eight nodes or locations. This corresponds to the number of *A*-types. And an *A*-type is a set of terms at the same location. Thus 'planet' is one *A*-type and 'heavy', 'large', 'red' is another.

The tree represents the permissible *way* of conjoining terms for significant sentences. If X and Y are terms at different locations on the tree, then $U(X, Y)$ if and only if either $X \leftarrow Y$ or $Y \leftarrow X$. If X and Y are at the same location, then $U(X, Y)$. On the other hand, if you cannot get from X to Y or from Y to X by a permitted path, then $N(X, Y)$. Since the 'paths' represent predicability, an N-pair or category mistake may be defined as a statement formed by conjoining two terms, *neither* of which is predicable of the other.

The tree structure is only a graphical representation of the tree rule. It illustrates graphically the fact that any natural language must have at least one term at the apex, a term defining a category which includes all other categories. Also, such a term is univocal; if it were not we would have to give it different locations. (It would be different 'terms' that have the same 'token'.) The tree structure makes clear that certain terms must be exclusive, defining categories which include no others.

Quine is therefore correct in his assertion that there can be 'no evidence' against anyone who wishes to place existence at the apex.

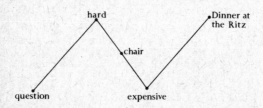

Furthermore, if there can be no evidence, then existence is univocal, since we accept a judgement of ambiguity only where it is logically enforceable. On the other hand, Quine is wrong in believing that we cannot *in general* get evidence for enforcing a judgement of ambiguity against a predicate that is predicated of things of different types. Thus he is wrong in saying that we can have no evidence for the ambiguity of 'hard' in the pairs (hard, chair) and (hard, question). The following values which violate the tree rule constitute logical evidence for the ambiguity of either 'hard' or 'expensive':

Figure II represents values inconsistent with the tree rule:

$$U(Q, H) \ U(H, E) \ N(Q, E) \ U(E, D) \ N(D, H).$$

These values cannot be placed on the tree structure. On the other hand, if we *split* the meaning of 'hard', giving that 'token' two type locations, we *can* dispose them on the tree.

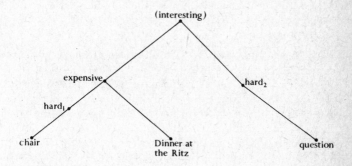

Thus the tree rule is a 'clarification rule', a 'univocity condition'.

Quine is wrong about 'hard' and right about 'exists'. Most other recent philosophers have been wrong about 'exists' and right about 'hard'. Neither Quine nor Black seems to have realized that there is a logical structure distributing the terms of a language for significant pairing,[1] and that unless a group of term pairs satisfies the structural condition, some of the terms are equivocal. Russell, in his *Reply*, hoped for such a structure, and he rightly believed that it would turn out to be hierarchical. He did not himself discover it because he was bound by the seductive transitivity rule for the *U*-relation.

---

[1] Indeed, Quine wishes to avoid a theory of types by classifying category mistakes as false 'and false by meaning, if one likes'. He believes this will 'spare us . . . both the settling of categories and the respecting of them'. But this also spares us all the benefits of a theory of types. And what can Quine mean by 'false by meaning'? Cf. *Word and Object*, p. 229. Quine's avoidance of type theory probably stems from the use of the transitivity rule together with the assumption that 'exists' is univocal. This gives the result that any two things are of the same type.

But transitivity, as we saw, leads to an impossible structure which ends by locating all the terms of a language at one 'node' and eliminating nonsensical pairs of terms altogether. Black, too, accepted the transitivity rule as the only possible one, and he concluded that the search for a type structure adequate for natural language was doomed, since too much ambiguity would then be generated. But the tree structure has the virtue of generating ambiguity where we want it and refraining from generating ambiguity where judgement of ambiguity would be counter-intuitive. Black's argument against the Russell programme is therefore voided as soon as we obtain a theory of types which provides a clarification rule that is not counter-intuitive.

I should like, in concluding, to list some of the advantages gained from recognizing the tree structure as a governing condition for natural languages:

> We obtain a satisfactory criterion for distinguishing the 'natural' subject of a proposition.
> We obtain a satisfactory clarification procedure for enforcing ambiguity at the type level.
> We obtain a clear algorithm for the isomorphism which holds between the distribution of sense and nonsense in a language and the distribution of categorial features in the world.
> We obtain a powerful technique for doing 'logical geography', what Ryle and others have sometimes identified with 'doing philosophy', though that is an overestimation of the importance of categorial analysis.
> We obtain a satisfactory explanation for the high incidence of grammatical nonsense in any natural language. A glance at the tree structure makes it clear that most pairs of terms must be N in sense value.

The structure has the merit of tying together two aspects of philosophy which for most philosophers have been sundered in recent years: the theory of predication and the theory of types. Thus the theory and the technique it gives us is essentially an Aristotelian development.

And, finally, it is clear that all languages have the same ontological structures in an important sense. Whatever 'sorts of things' a language discriminates, the notion of a sort remains the same and the sorting process is the same. At least this is so for any language containing expressions that we legitimately call 'predicates'.

APPENDIX: PROOF OF THE LAW OF CATEGORIAL INCLUSION

A sentence like 'Some philosophers are quaint' is said—in one sense of 'about'—to be about philosophers. In a second (categorial) sense, (P, Q) is about$_2$ whatever is either a philosopher or a non-philosopher. Thus (philosophers, quaint) is not about$_2$ Hopi rituals even though Hopi rituals are among things that are either quaint or not quaint. On the other hand, Hopi *Indians* are among the things that (P, Q) is about$_2$. We may formulate this as a definition for any P and Q.

D.1 $U(P\,Q) \equiv (P\,Q)$ is about$_2 |P| \lor (P\,Q)$ is about$_2 |Q|$.

Axiom: (A.1) Whatever $(P\,Q)$ is about$_2$ is in the universe of discourse of $(P\,Q)$.

Let '$V(P\,Q)$ stand for the universe of discourse of a sentence conjoining the terms P and Q, then

$$(x)\left[(x\epsilon\,V(P\,Q)) \equiv (x\epsilon |P|.|Q|)\right]$$

where $|P|.|Q|$ is the same as $(P \lor \bar{P})(Q \lor \bar{Q})$ which is the same as the familiar expression for the universe of discourse of (PQ), namely:

$$P.Q \lor P.\bar{Q} \lor \bar{P}.Q \lor \bar{P}.\bar{Q}$$

T.1 (The law of categorial inclusion)

$$U(P\,Q) \equiv (|P| \subset |Q|) \lor (|Q| \subset |P|)$$

Proof:

By A.1 and D.1 we have

$$
\begin{aligned}
U(P\,Q) &\equiv (|P| \subset V(PQ)) \lor (|Q| \subset V(P\,Q)) \\
&\equiv (|P| \subset |P|.|Q|) \lor (|Q| \subset |P|.|Q|) \\
&\equiv (|P| \subset |Q|) \lor (|Q| \subset |P|)
\end{aligned}
$$

Q.E.D.

NOTES ON THE CONTRIBUTORS

GOTTLOB FREGE (1848–1925) was a teacher of mathematics in the University of Jena. Though his writings were scarcely known during his lifetime except to those few logicians who shared his interests, he is now regarded as the principal founder of modern mathematical logic. His pamphlet *Begriffsschrift* appeared in 1879, the larger *Grundlagen der Arithmetik* in 1884, and the two volumes of his *Grundgesetze der Arithmetik* in 1893 and 1903. The *Grundlagen* has been published in an English translation by J. L. Austin (*Foundations of Arithmetic*, 2nd edn, 1953), and portions of the *Begriffsschrift* are included in a collection of his *Philosophical Writings*, translated by Max Black and P. T. Geach (1952).

H. P. GRICE is a Fellow of St. John's College, Oxford, and was William James Lecturer at Harvard in 1967.

MICHAEL DUMMETT is a Reader in the Philosophy of Mathematics at Oxford, and a Fellow of All Souls College.

P. F. STRAWSON, the editor of the present volume, is Waynflete Professor of Metaphysical Philosophy at Oxford, and was formerly a Fellow of University College there. His *Introduction to Logical Theory* was published in 1952, *Individuals: An Essay in Descriptive Metaphysics* in 1959, and *The Bounds of Sense* in 1966.

JOHN R. SEARLE is a Professor of Philosophy in the University of California at Berkeley. He has contributed many articles to philosophical periodicals, and is editing *The Philosophy of Language* in the present series.

D. F. PEARS is a Student of Christ Church, Oxford. He published in 1961, with B. F. McGuinness, a new translation of Wittgenstein's *Tractatus Logico-Philosophicus*, and his book *Bertrand Russell and the British Tradition in Philosophy* appeared in 1967.

JAMES THOMSON is Professor of Philosophy in the Department of Humanities, Massachusetts Institute of Technology.

ANTHONY QUINTON is a Fellow of New College, Oxford. He is the editor of *Political Philosophy* in the present series.

A. N. PRIOR, until recently Professor of Philosophy in the University of Manchester, is now a Fellow of Balliol College, Oxford. His *Logic and the Basis of Ethics* was published in 1949, *Formal Logic* in 1955, and *Time and Modality*, his John Locke Lectures, in 1957. His new book *Past, Present, and Future*, is to be published in 1967.

NUEL D. BELNAP is a member of the Department of Philosophy at the University of Pittsburgh.

FRED SOMMERS, formerly of Columbia, is now a member of the Philosophy Department at Brandeis University. He has written a number of articles in the field of philosophical logic.

BIBLIOGRAPHY

(not including material in this volume)

I. BOOKS

(1) *Classics of modern philosophical logic*

RUSSELL, B.: *Lectures on the Philosophy of Logical Atomism*, reprinted in Russell, *Logic and Knowledge*, ed. Marsh (Allen and Unwin, London, 1956).

WITTGENSTEIN, L.: *Tractatus Logico-Philosophicus*, trans. Pears and McGuinness (Routledge and Kegan Paul, London, 1961).

FREGE, G.: *Philosophical Writings*, trans. P. T. Geach and M. Black (Blackwell, Oxford, 1952).

(2) *Some recent books*

AUSTIN, J. L.: *Philosophical Papers* (Clarendon Press, Oxford, 1961). *How To Do Things With Words* (Clarendon Press, Oxford, 1962).

COHEN, L. J.: *The Diversity of Meaning* (Methuen, London, 1962).

GEACH, P. T.: *Reference and Generality* (Cornell University Press, Ithaca, N. Y., 1962).

PAP, A.: *Semantics and Necessary Truth* (Yale University Press, New Haven, Conn., 1958).

QUINE, W. V. O.: *From a Logical Point of View* (Harvard University Press, Cambridge, Mass., 1953).

Word and Object (Technology Press of the Massachusetts Institute of Technology and John Wiley and Sons, New York and London, 1960).

KNEALE, W. C.: *The Development of Logic* (Clarendon Press, Oxford, 1962).

STRAWSON, P. F.: *Introduction to Logical Theory* (Methuen, London, 1952).

II. TOPICS

(1) *Propositions, Assertion and Truth*

MOORE, G. E.: 'Beliefs and Propositions', and 'True and False Beliefs', *Some Main Problems of Philosophy*, Chapters XIV and XV (Allen and Unwin, London, 1953).

AUSTIN, J. L., and STRAWSON, P. F.: 'Truth', *Proceedings of the Aristotelian Society*, Supp. Vol. 1950; reprinted in *Truth*, ed. G. W. Pitcher (Contemporary Perspectives in Philosophy Series; Prentice Hall, Englewood Cliffs, N. J., 1964).

CARTWRIGHT, R.: 'Propositions', *Analytical Philosophy*, ed. R. J. Butler (Basil Blackwell, Oxford, 1962).

AYER, A. J.: 'Truth', *The Concept of a Person* (Macmillan, London, 1963).

WARNOCK, G. J. and STRAWSON, P. F.: 'A Problem about Truth', *Truth*, ed. G. W. Pitcher (Prentice-Hall, Englewood Cliffs, N. J., 1964).

STRAWSON, P. F.: 'Truth: A Reconsideration of Austin's Views', *Philosophical Quarterly* (1965).

GEACH, P. T.: 'Assertion', *Philosophical Review* (1965).

LEMMON, E. J.: 'Sentences, Statements and Propositions', *British Analytical Philosophy*, ed. B. A. O. Williams and A. C. Montefiore (Routledge and Kegan Paul, London, 1966).

(2) *Reference and Predication*

FREGE, G.: 'Sense and Reference', and 'Concept and Object', *Philosophical Writings*, trans. P. T. Geach and M. Black (Blackwell, Oxford, 1952).

RUSSELL, B.: *Lectures on the Philosophy of Logical Atomism* (Lectures II, III and VI) (*Logic and Knowledge*, Allen and Unwin, London, 1956).

AYER, A. J.: 'Names and Descriptions', *The Concept of a Person* (Macmillan, London, 1963).

QUINE, W. V. O.: *Word and Object* (Chapters III-V) (Massachusetts Institute, New York, 1960).

GEACH, P. T.: *Reference and Generality* (especially Chapter II) (Cornell University Press, Ithaca, 1962).

STRAWSON, P. F.: On Referring, *Mind* (1950), reprinted in *Essays in Conceptual Analysis*, ed. A. G. N. Flew (Macmillan, London, 1956).

Individuals (Chapters V and VI) (Methuen, London, 1959).

'Identifying Reference and Truth-Values', *Theoria* (1964).

DONNELLAN, K. S.: 'Reference and Definite Descriptions', *Philosophical Review* (1966).

AUSTIN, J. L.: 'How to Talk: Some Simple Ways', *Philosophical Papers* (Clarendon Press, Oxford, 1961).

(3) *Existence*

MOORE, G. E.: 'Is Existence a Predicate?', *Proceedings of the Aristotel-*

ian Society, Supp. Vol. (1936), reprinted in *Logic and Language*, Series II, ed. A. G. N. Flew (Basil Blackwell, Oxford, 1953).

CARNAP, R.: 'Empiricism, Semantics and Ontology', *Revue Internationale de Philosophie* (1950), reprinted in *Semantics and the Philosophy of Language,* ed. L. Linsky (University of Illinois Press, Urbana, 1952).

WARNOCK, G. J.: 'Metaphysics in Logic', *Proceedings of the Aristotelian Society* (1950–51).

QUINE, W. V. O.: 'On What There Is', *From a Logical Point of View* (Harvard University Press, Cambridge, Mass., 1953).

GEACH, P. T., AYER, A. J., and QUINE: 'On What There Is', *Proceedings of the Aristotelian Society*, Supp. Vol. (1951).

SCHEFFLER, I., and CHOMSKY, N.: 'What is said to be', *Proceedings of the Aristotelian Society* (1958–9).

STRAWSON, P. F.: *Individuals*, (Chapter VIII) (Methuen, London, 1959).

(4) Meaning and Use

GRICE, H. P.: 'The Causal Theory of Perception' (sections 2 to 4), *Proceedings of the Aristotelian Society*, Supp. Vol. (1961).

AUSTIN, J. L.: *How To Do Things With Words* (Clarendon Press, Oxford, 1962).

COHEN, L. J.: 'Do Illocutionary Forces Exist?'. *Philosophical Quarterly* (1964).

STRAWSON, P. F.: 'Intention and Convention in Speech-Acts', *Philosophical Review* (1964).

SEARLE, J. R.: 'Meaning and Speech-Acts', *Philosophical Review* (1962).

'What is a Speech Act?', *Philosophy in America*, ed. M. Black (Allen and Unwin, London, 1965).

'Assertions and Aberrations', *British Analytical Philosophy*, ed. B. A. O. Williams and A. C. Montefiore (Routledge and Kegan Paul, London, 1966).

WARNOCK, G. J.: 'Claims to Knowledge' (section II), *Proceedings of the Aristotelian Society* Supp. Vol. 1962, *pp*. 37–42.

(5) Conditionals

GOODMAN, N.: 'The Problem of Counterfactual Conditionals', *Fact, Fiction and Forecast*, Chapter 1 (Athlone Press, London, 1954).

QUINE, W. V. O.: *Methods of Logic*, Part I, Section 3 (Henry Holt, New York, 1950).

RYLE, G.: 'If, So and Because', *Philosophical Analysis*, ed. M. Black (Cornell University Press, Ithaca, N. Y., 1950).

VON WRIGHT, G. H.: 'On Conditionals', *Logical Studies* (Routledge and Kegan Paul, London, 1957).

RESCHER, N.: 'Belief-contravening Suppositions', *Philosophical Review* (1961).

MACKIE, J. L. 'Counterfactuals and Causal Laws', *Analytical Philosophy* ed. R. J. Butler (Basil Blackwell, Oxford, 1962).

(6) *Logical Constants, Logical Form, Logical Truth*

WITTGENSTEIN, L.: *Tractatus Logico-Philosophicus*, trans. and ed. D. F. Pears and B. F. McGuinness (Routledge and Kegan Paul, London, 1961).

POPPER, K. R.: 'Logic Without Assumptions', *Proceedings of the Aristotelian Society* (1946–7).

RYLE, G.: 'Formal and Informal Logic'. *Dilemmas* (Cambridge University Press, Cambridge, 1954).

PAP, A.: 'The Concept of Logical Truth', *Semantics and Necessary Truth*, Chapter VI (Yale University Press, New Haven, 1958).

STRAWSON, P. F.: 'Propositions, Concepts and Logical Truth', *Philosophical Quarterly* (1957)

(7) *Meaning and Necessity*

AYER, A. J.: 'The A Priori', *Language, Truth and Logic*, Chapter IV (2nd ed., Gollancz, London, 1946).

EWING, A. C.: 'The Linguistic Theory of A Priori Propositions', *Proceedings of the Aristotelian Society* (1939–40).

QUINE, W. V. O. 'Two Dogmas of Empiricism', *From a Logical Point of View* (Harvard University Press, Cambridge, Mass., 1953).

GRICE, H. P. and STRAWSON, P. F.: 'In Defence of a Dogma', *Philosophical Review* (1956).

BENNETT, J.: 'Analytic-Synthetic', *Proceedings of the Aristotelian Society* (1958–9).

PUTNAM: 'The Analytic and the Synthetic', *Minnesota Studies in the Philosophy of Science*, Vol. III (University of Minnesota Press, Minneapolis, 1962).

KNEALE, W. C.: 'Necessity and Language', *The Development of Logic*, Chapter X, Section 5 (Clarendon Press, Oxford, 1962).

(8) *Categories*

RYLE, G.: 'Categories', *Proceedings of the Aristotelian Society*, (1938–9), reprinted in *Logic and Language*, Series II, ed. A. G. N. Flew (Basil Blackwell, Oxford, 1953).

'Philosophical Arguments', reprinted in *Logical Positivism*, ed. A. J. Ayer (Free Press, Glencoe, Ill.; Allen and Unwin, London, 1959).

PASSMORE, J. A.: 'Allocation to Categories', *Philosophical Reasoning*, Chapter VII (Duckworth, London, 1961).

PAP, A.: 'Types and Meaninglessness', *Mind*, (1960).

SOMMERS, F.: 'Predicability', *Philosophy in America*, ed. M. Black (Allen and Unwin, London, 1965).

INDEX OF NAMES

(not including authors mentioned only in the Bibliography)

176